GENDERISMS, DECAPITATED AND SMASHED HEADS: AN ANALYSIS OF RICHARD WRIGHT'S MAJOR FICTION

YVONNE ROBINSON JONES

This book is a work of non-fiction. Unless otherwise noted, the author and the publisher make no explicit guarantees as to the accuracy of the information contained in this book and in some cases, names of people and places have been altered to protect their privacy.

Archway Publishing books may be ordered through booksellers or by contacting:

Archway Publishing
1663 Liberty Drive
Bloomington, IN 47403
www.archwaypublishing.com
844-669-3957

Because of the dynamic nature of the Internet, any web addresses or links contained in this book may have changed since publication and may no longer be valid. The views expressed in this work are solely those of the author and do not necessarily reflect the views of the publisher, and the publisher hereby disclaims any responsibility for them.

Any people depicted in stock imagery provided by Getty Images are models, and such images are being used for illustrative purposes only.
Certain stock imagery © Getty Images.

ISBN: 978-1-6657-4259-7 (sc)
ISBN: 978-1-6657-4260-3 (e)

Library of Congress Control Number: 2023907296

Print information available on the last page.

Archway Publishing rev. date: 07/31/2023

DEDICATION

This study is dedicated to my mother and father, the Late Sarah Westbrook Robinson and the late Omar Robinson Sr, and to my late siblings: Omar Jr., Elizabeth, Elsie, and Theodore (Prince), and James. Also, it is dedicated to my siblings who are still with me: Sam, Halloe, and Juanita, as well as my special niece Sonya. I have been very fortunate to have had the encouragement and support from my cousins, the Jones family and role models like those of the Westbrook clan. Their accomplishments, demonstrations of love and support have continued to motivate me in my professional pursuits. A special dedication is made to my supportive husband, the late John Eddie Jones, and my loving daughter, Sarah and to the matriarch of Richard Wright scholars, the late Margaret Walker Alexander. All have been comforting and uplifting.

ACKNOWLEDGMENTS

Thanks to Dr. Don Kartiganer, my director, for his patience and guidance throughout my research and writing, my committee members, Dr. Deborah Barker, Dr. Larry Hanshaw, and Dr. Ethel Young Minor, for their support and guidance. I am especially grateful for the encouragement I received from my colleagues at Southwest Tennessee Community College: administrators, staff, and especially the librarians and faculty across all disciplines. I am grateful for the typing and editorial assistance from Lubecca Douglas, Verneta Boone, John Speed, Mary Wilkinson, and Dr. Andrew Kelley. The inspiration and support of friends, Carolyn Bell, Sandra Burke, Billy Gholson, Charlene Price, Lillie Jackson, Rose McNeil, Evelyn Little, Stennis Trueman, Carolyn and Wendell Coward, and the late Drs. Richard and Evelyn Carroll, my Spelman mentors, who will always be remembered. A special acknowledgment is made to Dr. Maryemma Graham, the late Dr. Colby Kullman, Dr. Roseanne Bell, and the late Dr. Miriam Decosta Willis. Their mentoring and support continue to strengthen me in my literary and professional engagements. A special thanks to Julie Dockery and Kya Reeves for their fresh insights as the next generation of scholars.

VITA

Yvonne Robinson Jones was born in Memphis, Tennessee and is Professor Emeritus of Fine Arts, Languages and Literature at Southwest Tennessee Community College in Memphis, Tennessee. Jones completed her bachelor's degree from Spelman College, her master's from The University of Oregon, and Ph.D. from The University of Mississippi with an emphasis in American and African American Literature. She became the founding Director of International and Study Abroad Programs at Southwest Tennessee Community College. Naomi Tutu and Julia Wright, the daughter of Richard Wright, were her Program opening speakers.

Jones has done extensive research in the life and texts of Richard Wright and directed the project for a multi-media program that included a free-standing pictorial exhibit on permanent display in the Parrish Library of Southwest, visiting speakers, panel discussions, as well as discovered the first *Native Son* film starring Wright as Bigger. The project was funded by Humanities Tennessee.

Because of Jones' interest in ethnic studies and diversity, she became a participant in an Ethnic Heritage seminar and studied in four countries in West Africa: Senegal, The Gambia, Mali, and Liberia. She joined the first community of scholars to travel to Paris, France to honor Richard Wright and other African American writers who have lived as expatriates there. Also, she studied in Cairo, Egypt as a Fulbright Scholar focusing on Islamic and Egyptian culture, religion, and literature. Having taught Hispanic and African American literature, she was a presenter at the International Symposium on Global Languages and Literature, sponsored by the National Council for Teachers of English hosted by The University of Utrecht in Utrecht, The Netherlands.

Jones was a contributing writer for the first African American Literature anthology for high school students, *African American Literature, Voices in a Tradition*. Throughout her academic and professional career Jones has presented at conferences locally, nationally, and internationally. Having taught at all levels in higher education, she has assisted in the development of African American literature and cultural diversity courses for Southwest Tennessee Community College, The University of Memphis, and The University of Mississippi. For her efforts in teaching, she received the Chancellor's Diversity Award from The National Endowment for the Humanities, the Outstanding Professional Growth and Development Award from Southwest Tennessee Community College, and The Outstanding Educator's Award from Alpha Phi Alpha Fraternity at The University of Mississippi. She has participated in activities sponsored by several community organizations in the Memphis and Nashville areas throughout her professional career: Humanities Tennessee, Memphis in May International Festival, Inc., Leadership Memphis, and Community Health Resources. The Urban Arts Committee's Artist Participation Committee is her latest endeavor, a mayoral appointment. As a retiree, she is a volunteer for The Brooks Museum League of the Memphis Brooks Museum and became its first African American President in 2011.

FOREWORD

My earliest memory of my mother's residence as a doctoral student at The University of Mississippi was my enrollment in daycare because of a picture of me there. But the most exciting moment for me while there was attending the musical "Into the Woods" starring Marilyn McCoo of the Fifth Dimension. There was a large pair of sunglasses on stage I would have loved to own, and at the age of five I felt my mother could make anything happen. She, along with my grandmothers and all of my aunts, were strong, adorable women who shaped both of our lives including that of my father, the late John Eddie Jones.

I had a very strong and supportive father who was a Medical Photographer at The University of Tennessee Center for the Health Sciences, UTCHS, in Memphis, Tennessee. He later became a Fine Arts Professor at The Memphis College of Art and Southwest Tennessee Community College where he and my mother taught. They had a matriculating marriage, while we were living in graduate student housing at The University of Mississippi in Oxford, Mississippi, approximately 75 miles south of Memphis. My mother had taken a leave of absence from her college, Southwest, to begin her doctoral study after receiving a National Endowment for the (NEH) graduate faculty fellowship. She proposed to study the texts of Richard Wright not only as an African American writer, but a southern one, born and bred in the South and imbued with the motivation to reveal a racially divided America that victimized black people both male and female.

My mother's friends and family were aware of her unrelenting interest in Wright, as well as her desire to do further graduate study because she had already begun to engage in several major projects on the writer;

she had taken several undergraduate and graduate courses in African American literature where she read Black Boy (1945) and realized he lived in Memphis as a young boy and adult. He graduated as valedictorian of Smith Robertson school in Jackson, Mississippi, had come to Memphis with his parents, was left by his father, and later placed in a CME orphanage by his mother. Wright's journey was traced and photographically presented in a free standing exhibit my mother developed, with it traveling throughout the city and to states with included lecturers at various library sites. She acquired a reputation as a Richard Wright scholar and exalted his works and his legacy. *Native Son* (1940) and *Black Boy* became bestsellers that certainly catapulted Wright's career.

I recall asking my mother if God could be a woman. Her answer was, "God can be an It, a male, and yes a female." We both laughed. Strong, funny, and loving women surrounded me, and as I continued my childhood education, I recall seeing my mother's books on gender, women novelists, African American writers and, of course, Richard Wright. More importantly, when my mother was Director of International Studies at Southwest, I remember Julia Wright, the writer's daughter, as one of her program speakers. I was a student at Spelman College in Atlanta, Georgia at the time, but I always kept abreast of my mother's and father's artsy engagements. I recalled meeting other Wright scholars in Mississippi: Dr. Maryemma Graham and the renowned Dr. Margaret Walker Alexander whose *Richard Wright: Demonic Genius* sits among so many books of my father and mother in their home library. My father, the late J. Eddie Jones, provided the photographs for Alexander's publication.

Genderisms, Decapitated and Smashed Heads: An analysis of Wright's Major Fiction is the result of my encouraging my mother to publish her dissertation. She responded, "The program is challenging but fun. My students, my classes, my international studies duties, and my duties as a mother and wife have my attention as well." Primarily, my mother is late bloomer; she had me at 40, she even married in her late 20's, and began her doctoral studies when I was 9 months old sitting in a car seat in the back of her light blue 1985 Saab. In addition, she always did overseas travel abroad, and her serious and studious demeanor awarded her fellowships and educational opportunities: a Fulbright in Cairo, Egypt to study Islamic Literature, to read a paper at the University of Utrecht, to participate in an Ethnic Heritage Seminar in West Africa, to meet anthology publication deadlines and, of course, her doctoral studies. There were other older students in the doctoral program. Some had children my age older. I was the youngest, and we all had so much fun bonding during that time.

This publication, Gen*derisms, Decapitated and Smashed Heads: An Analysis of Richard Wright's Major Fiction*, is a gem in my mother's academic crown that family, friends, the late J.Eddie Jones, my father, and other loving ancestral spirits are proud of and embrace.

Sarah Anna Elizabeth Jones

ABSTRACT

"Decapitated and Smashed Heads: A Gender-Based Study of Richard Wright's Major Fiction" cites a pattern termed the "use and discard" of the female character—a pattern that results from a narrative technique Wright uses to present the plight of the African American male in a historically racially divided society. Wright's pattern of the use and discard of female characters is examined in major novels and short stories with male-centered dynamics. These dynamics create the sexism and misogyny often discussed in Wright feminist and gender criticism. This analysis of the pattern demonstrates how the female is a catalyst for dramatic action and conflicts engaging African American males. Also, the study presents how the pattern of "use and discard" occurs in male and female relationships, in male bonding or male homosocial scenarios, in Wright's characterization of the white female character, and in his treatment of his most prominent protagonist, Bigger Thomas in *Native Son*. The female character is pivotal to the narrative structure of Wright's fiction in creating its plots and subplots. However, once the female's purpose has been fulfilled by Wright, she is no longer needed; she is repudiated, discarded, and often killed, such as in the cases of Mary Dalton and Bessie Mears, major female characters in *Native Son*. The subjugation of the female and the widely cited sexism and misogyny in Wright's fiction, its phallogocentrism, are acknowledged in the study. The analysis extends beyond the existing Wright feminist and gender-oriented criticism and examines how this pattern of use and discard occurs as a narrative technique Wright uses to achieve his artistic goals with his male characters.

PREFACE

"I always felt that brick beating against my head" is a comment Alice Walker made while discussing her novel, *The Color Purple,* and her motivation for writing it. Though Walker was speaking both literally (the brick Bigger uses to kill Bessie in *Native Son*) and symbolically (the sexism and misogyny in male texts, particularly those of Wright), the brick image became a fixation for me as well, while journeying through the texts of Richard Wright. However, even before Walker's comments were heard and began to resonate in my mind, I always remembered a literature seminar at Spelman College where I encountered Doris Lessing's *Golden Notebooks.* My female colleagues and I were introduced to a type of discourse, a feminist one, that would reshape and change every perspective we held on the plight of women in male-oriented and dominated societies, particularly our own, the American society. Therefore, this introduction to a feminist reading of texts became the basis for my subsequent interest in using a gender-oriented approach in analyzing Richard Wright's fiction.

As African American females, my peers and I developed in so many ways, especially intellectually, and became quite accustomed to analyzing and critiquing the race factor in our lives and those of African American people. After all, it was the 1960s, and we were encouraged to view matters in terms of race. Also, after reading *Black Boy*, I was compelled to think dichotomously, for every element of society, especially television, was continuously presenting images, dialogues, and speeches that focused on a racially divided society while, simultaneously, proclaiming integration.

In the 1970s, I revisited *Black Boy* and was introduced to Wright's other major texts, *Uncle Tom's Children* (1938), *Native Son* (1940), and

The Outsider (1953). It was *Black Boy* that caused me to view Wright not only as an African American writer but a southern one—born and bred in the Mid-South and living briefly, on two occasions, in my hometown, Memphis, Tennessee. By the end of the 1970s, Memphis was most popularly known as a blues and music town, with Beale Street, as well as Stax and Sun Records recording companies, producing such greats as W. C. Handy, Elvis Presley, Otis Redding, and B.B. King. However, few scholars had focused on the role Memphis played in shaping some of the country's most prominent writers—William Faulkner, Tennessee Williams, and Richard Wright, who was eventually considered as the father of the Black Protest Novel.

As a result of my reading and studying Wright's major texts, I was motivated to share with audiences the regional influences of the South that provide the context for his art. Wright's texts revised not only the African American literary canon in the 1940s but also contributed to mainstream American literature, as well, producing two bestsellers in a five-year span, *Native Son* in 1940 and *Black Boy* in 1945. Both texts have regional significance, the former presenting the plight of African Americans living in depressed northern urban centers as a result of their transmigration from the South to the North during the Great Migration of the 1920s, and the latter reflecting the violence and racism targeting African American communities in the South, especially African American males.

After producing a multimedia project that presented Wright as a product of the Mid-South—Mississippi, Tennessee, and Arkansas—I began to see the writer more comprehensively—not simply as a southern African American and Marxist one, which Wright criticism explores in depth, but a writer whose works have been compared to a prism, defined as a "polyhedron, used for separating *white light* (my own italics) passed into a spectrum" (*The American Heritage Dictionary*, third edition). The prism is an appropriate symbol for Richard Wright's art, for while it produces this singular effect on the racial divide in America and global communities, it simultaneously projects *other rays of thought* to reflect the complexities of the human experience and, especially, the myriad drama that unfolds in a region with a history of racial conflict.

This celebration of Wright in a regional context led me to the French feminists, Helene Cixous, Luce Irigaray, and Julia Kristeva, who informed me of a feminist analysis that cites the use and patterns of language, a linguistic approach, to examine the phallogocentrism in texts. In addition, since the misogyny in Wright's fiction is so apparent, a substantive body of criticism treating such was well established by the 90s. However, it was not until I read Nagueyalti Warren's essay, "Black Girls and Native Son: Female Images in Selected Works by Richard Wright," that the thought of using another approach, a feminist/gender one, was considered. Warren urges feminist critics to go beyond those existing pedestrian studies in her claim that "it is not enough ... merely to allude to sexism or explain it as the norm for a particular historical period" (59). Thus, this critic's position on the role of feminist criticism became the motivation for my subsequent reading of Wright's fiction and examining it beyond those pedestrian studies. I searched further than the familiar analyses and retrieved Wright feminist and gender-oriented criticism utilizing poststructuralist approaches, as well as more recent gender theories.

A thorough examination of Wright's texts will reveal the overt presentation of racial conflict, with the action primarily centering on the victimization of African American males. Also, historically, Wright's fiction has been the target of criticism that often focuses on its violent, psycho-sexual, propagandist, and misogynist effects. However, the 1970s signaled a more specific gender approach to Wright in feminist criticism, citing, in so many instances, not only the unwarranted harsh treatment of female characters but the horrific circumstances regarding their demise: murder and decapitation (Mary Dalton in *Native Son*), rape and murder (Bessie in *Native Son*), suicide (Eva in the *Outsider*), as well as death by childbirth (LuLu in "Down By the Riverside"). The litany of horrible deaths Wright's female characters incur is chilling evidence of an artist who crafts females in horrific and repulsive images while, simultaneously, presenting a scathing indictment of American racism. Moreover, with most Wright criticism approaching such analyses from sociocultural and historical perspectives, one will observe that this approach begins to wane in the latter part of the twentieth century with more recent critical studies (80s and 90s) engaging critical and gender theories treating Wright's texts in another critical context, i.e., another language, which is not simply a story of Wright's most historic protagonist in *Native Son,* Bigger Thomas.

Writer and critic, Sherley A. Williams, makes an interesting comment that points to past treatments of Wright's fiction in the statement, "We excuse these characterizations (of women) because of the power of Wright's psychological portrait of Bigger" (397). A critical assessment that presents a similar perspective in Wright feminist criticism is that of Alan W. France's "Misogyny and Appropriation in Wright's *Native Son,*" which alludes to the French feminists and uses a poststructuralist approach. France's position, as well as that of Warren and Williams, is an excellent departure point for examining Wright beyond the familiar borders. He states, "It is time to revoke these privileges accorded to (the author) and to recover the radical alterity in the text that reduces women to property, valuable only to the extent they serve as objects of phallocentric status conflicts. If read as the negative polarity of the text, this process of male reification and appropriation pervades the work" (414). Moreover, France's analysis provided valuable assistance in giving me "the eye" for the reading and research I needed to formulate my own theoretical frame for a study of female characters in Wright's fiction. In addition in "Richard Wright's Women Characters and Inequality," Sylvia Keady observes that "female characters frequently function as *vehicles* (my italics) through which the hero's problems and difficulties are further increased" (124).

Keady's assessment cohered with my own observations, and after perceiving the female utilized as a conduit for Wright's phallocentric objectives, I began to peruse the texts further, searching for a dynamic that would take me beyond even that referent. At this point in my reading and research, I began to see a pattern with Wright's vehicular use of the female character—a pattern that I have termed the "use and discard" of the female as a result of the writer's narrative technique—a structural crafting—that facilitates his purpose with the male protagonist. Wright accomplishes his artistic end—that of presenting to readers the plight of African American males in a racialized capitalist society—by using the female as catalyst (used in a literary context) to set off the dramatic action, the narrative conflict. Once this is achieved, the female character is no longer needed for the writer's artistic purpose. Therefore, she is discarded, cast off, and phallocentric interests prevail; the needs of a male, not a *female*, protagonist take center stage. This pattern exists in primarily all of Wright's major and even minor fictional texts and is an operative for the writer's narrative structure.

At the end of my study, I encountered revealing evidence to reiterate the credence of this pattern of use and discard with the female character. In an interview of the prominent Wright biographer, Margaret Walker Alexander, she mentions her role of providing the sociology for Wright's *Native Son* and discusses the challenges she faced in writing and publishing her biography of Wright, *Richard Wright: Daemonic Genius* (1988). As a result of a widely publicized incident that caused her friendship with the writer to end in New York in 1939, she is questioned about the occurrence. Her comment was an epiphany for me regarding my particular study, for she states, "I guess he used and discarded me." Thus, Walker Alexander's perception of her professional relationship with Wright reflects the approach he uses in characterizing females for the development of fictional narratives that focus primarily on the victimization of African American male characters.

Two conceptual theories I found germane to this concept of use and discard are those espoused in Judith Fetterly's *The Resisting Reader* and Donald Grenier's *Women Enter the Wilderness: Male Bonding and the American Novel of the 1980s*. Fetterley's notion of female abandonment and Grenier's theory of male bonding as a requisite for such provided strong support for my argument's analysis of how Wright's artistic technique demonstrates this particular pattern of use and discard. The female character is intrinsic to his artistic purpose when it is grounded in phallocentric conflicts. In other words, behind every Wrightsian plot with an African American male is usually a quintessential female, African American or white. In addition to the texts of Fetterley and Grenier are those of Edith Sedgwick and Leslie Fielder. Both Sedgwick's and Fieldler's studies provide the appropriate apparatus for the analysis of homosocialism or male bonding and, especially, homosocial desire and eroticism as a result of the female's pivotal function in the narrative's structure.

A major contribution to this particular study and also to the field of feminist and critical studies is Alice Walker's womanist theory, which is another appropriate context for examining African American male and female characterizations more holistically in texts, especially those reflecting the triad oppression of African American females in terms of race, sex, and class. Williams prefers "womanist" as an appropriate concept because she finds that the definition is "'committed to the survival and wholeness of entire people' (Walker), female and male, as well as to a valorization of women's works in all their varieties and multitudes" (qtd. in Williams 70). Regarding male texts and their portraitures of women, especially African American male texts' imaging of African American females, Williams contends: "Womanist inquiry assumes that it can talk both effectively and productively about men. This is a necessary assumption because the negative, stereotyped images of black women are only part of the problem of phallocentric writings by black males. In order to understand the problem more fully, we must turn to what black men have written about themselves" (70). A similar position regarding a more inclusionary approach in feminist criticism is the position of Lillian Robinson regarding the tendency of traditional feminist criticism to be solely politically and academically centered on women's writing. To Robinson, ". . . while not abandoning our new-found female tradition, we have to return to confrontation with 'the' canon, examining it as a source of ideas, themes, motifs, and myths about the two sexes. The point in so doing is not to label and hence dismiss even the most sexist literary classics, but to enable all of us to apprehend them, finally, in all their human dimensions" (223). Thus, to define Richard Wright's sexism and misogyny in the language of this pattern of use and discard is to present another analytical approach that continues the development and enhancement of existing Wright feminist criticism and gender studies.

The womanist approach not only entails female treatment but also male, for, as Williams and Robinson suggest, it is necessary to capture the full dimension of the author's treatment of both sexes in order to illumine one.

Thus, chapter one examines the situation of the female and her vital role as the narrative unfolds, however, in the context of male/female relations. Also, the male-to-male relations become quite pertinent in providing the rationale for female repudiation and discard and are often the context for emphasizing the pivotal functions and demise of female characters as discussed in my second chapter. And even though Wright criticism is often grounded in the symbolic relationship of Bigger and the most prominent white female character, Mary Dalton, there are other white female characters in Wright's fiction that evidence this pattern of use and discard. Chapter three, therefore, analyzes Wright's treatment of the white female character as she enters and exits his narratives, having functioned as either a villainous catalyst for dramatic conflict or a naïve innocent one caught in circumstances that culminate in tragedy. This chapter also elucidates the commodious nature of black and white female lives, by citing the case of Bessie Mears who prevails as the most prominent of Wright's African American female characters, exploited and castigated, and whose murder is *literally* a case of discard in *Native Son*; she is thrown down an air shaft.

While utilizing more recent concepts and theories for examining Wright's treatment of female characters, I have also found it necessary to allude to traditional sociocultural and historical interpretations. Margaret Walker Alexander's *Daemonic Genius* proved to be most valuable in complementing the analysis of Wright's narrative technique, especially with the fourth and final chapter on Bigger Thomas where the homoerotic and Wright's feminine self are explored. This analysis of the Wright and Bigger relationship parallels some aspects of how Walker Alexander perceives Wright's artistic sensibility as a result of the author's familial conflicts and, more important, challenges and confrontations experienced in a racially polarized and threatening South of the early 1900s. In addition, Miriam Decosta Willis's response to the structuralist and poststructuralist approaches support the sociocultural and historical interpretation. Decosta Willis argues:

> . . . . in spite of the dictum of many contemporary scholars
> that literary texts must be read in isolation, the novels of

> Afro-American writers, particularly those, like Wright, who call themselves naturalists or social realists, must be read within the socio-economic and historical contexts in which the works were produced. (541)

The context for Wright's fiction, a racialized and life-threatening environment, is so compelling that in order to grasp the totality of the writer's artistic consciousness, one is hard pressed to exclude the sociocultural and historical. Even Houston Baker, whose critical approaches are often viewed as poststructural and deconstructionist, admits that in order to fully comprehend Wright's text, one must consider the autobiographical sources. Because of the fecundity of gender issues Wright's texts pose, one recent study that utilizes the deconstructionist approach of Michel's Foucault's *The History of Sexuality* is that of Abdul JanMohamed, whose treatment of sexuality in Wright's *Native Son* revises earlier interpretations of African American male and white female relations in the novel. One recent and fresh contribution to Wright feminist and gender criticism is Neal A. Lester's observation of a warped notion of sexuality in the form of sexual aggression and sexual violence (too often glorified in popular culture) in the lyrics of gangster rap. Lester cites this similar pathology in Wright's concept of sexuality and the mythology of the African American male rapist phenomenon in the short story, "The Man Who Killed a Shadow." These types of studies are timely and necessary for creating complementary and alternative schools of thought in Wright criticism for readers, students, and scholars who are attracted to the richness and complexity of this writer's art. By analyzing this pattern of use and discard of the female character in Wright's fiction, I have explored other realms of the writer's narrative technique and artistic strategy. Finally, the entire exercise of researching and reading the substantive body of feminist and gender criticism on Wright, as well as becoming acquainted with the various theories in gender studies has been rewarding. This entire study has spawned many other thoughts and possibilities for revisiting the texts of such an intriguing and challenging writer.

Yvonne Robinson Jones

CONTENTS

CHAPTER 1

Femaleness In The Maleness Of Richard Wright's Fiction

> I am launching out upon another novel, this time about the status of women in modern American society. This book, too, goes back to my childhood just as Bigger went, for while I was storing away impressions of Bigger, I was storing away impressions of many other things that made me think and wonder. ("How 'Bigger' Was Born," *Native Son* 461)

Richard Wright's protagonist, Bigger Thomas, in Wright's best-seller novel, *Native Son* (1940) has intrigued readers for decades, resulting in a plethora of criticism focusing on the text and Wright's motivation for creating the character. Bigger joined a litany of African American males who had been introduced to audiences in Wright's highly acclaimed collection of short fiction, *Uncle Tom's Children* (1938). Thus, the above passage in which Wright expresses an interest in women is rather ironic since he primarily uses the African American male as a vehicle for protest and, in doing so, unfavorably images females, particularly African American. This particular passage is also novel since Wright is equating his interest in women with his interest in Bigger, who prevailed not only as his most historic protagonist but the one who catapulted his literary career. Wright's female characters, however, certainly cannot share the center stage with his African American males, who are so often the target of racial hatred

1

and conflict in his narratives. But they do serve an important function in Wright's male-centered texts; they become vital in formulating initial conflict and drama. After functioning in this capacity, their presence and significance eventually wanes because they are subsumed by the dynamics of Wright's males' sojourn in a racially divided and patriarchal American society.

Wright's use of the phrase "think and wonder" in the passage suggests that he stood in awe of woman as subject.[1] And just as Wright's awe with the Bigger persona in Mississippi led to a major contribution to American literature with Bigger Thomas, one could speculate that a comparable woman could have led to the creation of a female character, more than likely an African American one, who would capture the attention of readers and critics as Bigger had. But this assumption is hypothetical, and Wright's texts speak for themselves. With Wright's fiction being primarily male-centered, it is needless to say that a noticeable interest in women never became realized in his fiction, despite his intentions to write about them as indicated in the aforementioned quote.

Regardless of Wright's intentions, his texts have provoked a monolithic school of feminist criticism that generally views him as a misogynist, whose negative and stereotypical imaging of women is explicit and unredeeming. Such criticism tends to be minimally varied in critical approaches, but recent feminist and gender approaches to analyzing Wright's texts are being utilized. Miriam Decosta Willis defends the sociocultural and historical approach in "Avenging Angels and Mute Mothers: Black Southern Women in Wright's Fictional World." Decosta Willis argues, ". . . Wright's consideration of women must begin with the writer's own experiences, attitudes, and feelings, for, in spite of the dictum of many contemporary scholars that literary texts must be read in isolation, the novels of African American writers, particularly those like Wright, who call themselves naturalist or social realists, must be read within the socio-economic and historical contexts in which the works were produced" (541). However, one critic who recognizes a need for a metamorphosis in Wright feminist criticism is Jane Davis, who claims that an "examination of Wright's version of women in general—both black and white—is necessary, going beyond the question of whether Wright portrays stereotypical black female characters" (60).

Davis's claim is timely because it makes an appeal for a more thorough and extensive treatment of Wright's female characters; such needed treatment will go beyond the criticism that simply analyzes the stereotyping and sexism and will examine more definitively those obvious characterizations and, too, those phallogocentric subtleties that should be addressed. Perhaps Nagueyalti Warren's comments also aptly assess this need in the statement, "it is not enough to allude to sexism or explain it as the norm for a particular historical period. It is necessary to examine the images, to expose the motivation for them, and to understand their insidious effects, if lifelike images are ever to emerge" (59). In addition, Joyce Ann Joyce's *The Art of Richard Wright's Tragedy* solicits critical approaches that utilize the New Criticism and more contemporary literary theory. She cites a stasis in Wright criticism since it fails to utilize structuralist and poststructuralist approaches. Joyce's views anticipate more recent feminist, gender, and womanist criticism, which offer alternative philosophical and theoretical contexts for examining Wright's narrative technique and motivation for his characterization of females.

An examination of Wright's criticism in the latter twentieth century reveals that Wright feminist scholarship does include postsructuralist and deconstructionist schools of thought and recent gender theories. Also, a cadre of feminist Wright criticism has been influenced by the French feminist school, alluding to either Helen Cixous, Luce Irigaray, or Julia Kristeva, as well as deconstructionists like Michel Foucault. For example, Alan W. France's "Misogyny and Appropriation in Wright's *Native Son*" draws on more recent gender theory to present what he calls a dialectical subtext in *Native Son*. By using Cixous's concept of "the realm of the proper" and Toril Moi's "the expropriated man," France's analysis examines the patriarchal nature of the novel; he examines the center stage afforded to Bigger by not only Wright but his critics as well. The critic examines Wright's underlying subtext by utilizing Cixous's and Moi's concepts and argues against a male-centered approach often brought to Wright's fiction, suggesting that Wright's treatment of female characters has finally found another context for examination—one that reveals how the female characters are appropriated in the text. Also, in response to another view that critically cites Wright's authorial control—"this is Bigger's story" (Shirley Anne Williams 397)—France contends that "it is time now to revoke these privileges accorded Bigger and to recover the radical alterity in the text that reduces women to property, valuable only to the extent they serve as objects of phallocentric status conflicts." France further contends, "this process of male reification and appropriateness pervades the work" (414).

In addition to France, Abdul R. JanMohamed's "Sexuality on/of the Racial Border: Wright and the Articulation of Racialized Sexuality" is an analysis of Michel Foucault's theory of sexuality and definition of power and its application to *Native Son*.[2] JanMohamed focuses on Bigger's rape charge regarding the white Mary Dalton, and in applying the concept of "racialized sexuality" differentiates Bessie's rape and murder from the murder and alleged rape of Mary. Along with JanMohamed's criticism are those theories and concepts emanating from black feminist and womanist criticism, both addressing the triad oppression of women of color: sex, color, and class. In addition, because of its failure to overtly address issues and concerns regarding women of color, traditional feminist criticism has been viewed by black feminists or more recent gender theorists as being just as exclusionary as the phallogocentrism of their male counterparts.[3] Thus, some feminists in the United States, particularly those of color, rejected Euro-American and European feminist criticism and created their own philosophical and political concepts that deal with gender issues and their connection to "race and class." Womanist theory primarily ensued, not necessarily as a reactionary mode of thought, but a complementary one to those schools of feminism that were deemed exclusionary. Thus, a shift occurred in black feminist thought (1980s), causing a reevaluation of its position, and the term womanism and womanist was coined by Alice Walker in her first collection of essays, *In Search of Our Mother's* Gardens. Walker defines womanist as "a black feminist" or feminist of color, one who views the situation of females in terms of color and class, as well as gender; she argues that unlike females, African American, Native American,

Asian, and Latino women, historically, have been victimized in western communities. This victimization has occurred not only because they were female but also because they were not Caucasian females; therefore, they view their victimization more as a consequence of race and class, first, and, secondly, gender.

Conversely, though, for some women of color, their gender is a primary cause of victimization in their own homogenous and patriarchal communities, and the victimization of their male counterparts has often been the cause of this victimization. Regardless, the triad of oppression—race, class, and gender—creates the premise from which black feminist and womanist thought evolves. A perfect target for this mode of analysis is Wright's characterization of Bessie in *Native Son*. Aside from Bessie being victimized by Bigger, who intimidates, frightens, and murders her because of his own troubling complexities (and his own victimization by the larger society), she too is victimized by the economic and social constructs of the larger society, e.g., working long hours for low wages, historically the situation of the African American domestic.

A close examination of Wright's treatment of the female character has revealed that though she is stereotyped, she is a necessary agent in the narratorial process. The female character becomes a vital operative in her relationship with Wright's male characters. It is her pivotal status in most of Wright's fiction that is the stimulus, the catalyst, for establishing the narrative's plot, its major conflict. The nexus of Wright feminist criticism is how he stereotypes and subjugates the female, yet the technique or design for executing the process of marginalizing and subjugating her is another crucial aspect of his fiction that requires further examination. The dynamics of male/female relationships will reveal that though the female character is negated, she is a needed agent in the artistic process. And proceeding from her vital position in Wright's narrative and phallic-centered conflict is her repudiation, castigation, and, finally, her discard. This chapter will examine Wright's fiction as it presents this particular function of the female character's use and discard in her relations and relationships with Wright's male characters, in most instances, his male protagonist.

Concomitant with France's observations of the female subtext in the phallogocentrism of Wright's *Native Son* is Judith Fetterley's conceptual frame presented in *The Resisting Reader*, which cites the contradictions surrounding the male/female relationship in Washington Irving's "Rip Van Winkle" and other male texts. Fetterley analyzes the functions of a male world that are empowered by the "immasculation" of the female. "Immasculation" is the term she uses to define the process by which women are undermined, stereotyped, objectified, and subjugated. Interestingly, the term, "emasculation," is most often used to define the racial oppression of Wright's males; however, it becomes "immascuation" to define the subjugation of females in male texts according to Fetterley. France's idea of a dialectical subtext in *Native Son* and Fetterley's treatment of male texts that convey the contradictions and reversals in male/female roles in American society are useful for examining male/female relations because there exists in Wright's fiction a dialectical pattern involving the acceptance and rejection of the female, when, as France has observed, phallocentric interests arise, i.e., male affairs and conflict resolution. In the process woman is accepted and then rejected. However, regardless of the extent to which Wright subjugates and negates females, an even closer observation of the male/female dynamic will reveal her necessity, as well as her exploitation and eventual repudiation and discard. She is vital in serving the needs of males and Wright's artistic purpose, which is primarily to inform the reading public of American racism that particularly targets American males. The female is a means to this end, and once Wright's artistic objective has been met, she is discarded, simply thrown away.

Wright recognized this need of woman, as he termed it, "her status in modern American society." Since the female is at the center of Wrightsian conflict, she is the agent that is responsible for initiating the rising action in the narrative. Females provide Wright with some form of racial conflict needed to demonstrate the plots and subplots that will subsequently convey his themes of protest; in essence, females help him achieve his artistic goal(s).

An examination of Wright's major fiction will reveal this narrative technique that posits the female as crucial to his narrative structure.

Beginning with the autobiographical *Black Boy*, a female boarder, Ella, introduces young Richard to his first fictional text, interestingly, *The Tales of Blue Beard*, and against the wishes of his religiously fanatical grandmother. Young Wright is literally mesmerized by the tale, and as Wright, the autobiographer, recalls the incident, he states, "the world became peopled with magic presences" (45). Once Wright experiences this magic of fiction, his imagination is sparked, and he thirsts for more; he asks his mother to teach him to read. She agrees and, thus, females are Wright's first literary nurturers as he embarks on his path to literacy; they precede male novelists like Theodore Dreiser and Fyodor Doestoyevsky, who will eventually become shapers of his literary sensibility.

One female character that dominates Wright criticism is Mary Dalton in Wright's 1940 bestseller, *Native Son*. The protagonist, Bigger Thomas, accidentally kills Mary Dalton, a white girl, by smothering her with a pillow. His innocent gesture to put Mary to bed because of a drunken stupor sets off a chain of events and reactions involving the tabooed African American male and white female relationship. This gives the narrative its jarring and controversial appeal. But juxtaposed with Mary's murder is Bigger's intentional murder of Bessie, his girlfriend, whom he hits over the head with a brick and throws down an air shaft to die. However, it is obvious that Bigger's murder of white Mary is more important in the novel and the one that causes the most controversy. Thus, Bigger's murder of Bessie and Wright's de-emphasis of it not only exacerbates Bigger's brutishness, but it also inculcates the difference of value in black and white life—the stuff that Wright's artistic demons love to create. Bigger's initial encounter and murder of Mary provide the main plot and action in *Native Son*. Wright is "doing his thing," but observe the price both female characters have to pay, not to mention Bigger's mother, whom he verbally abuses, and his little sister, Vera, who is victimized by Bigger's playful and sadistic gesturing in the famous rat scene at the beginning of the novel.

In Wright's short fiction collection and first literary achievement, *Uncle Tom's Children*, Lulu's death-threatening labor pains in "Down by the Riverside" not only create the central conflict but present the burden that puts her husband and the entire African American community at risk. Mann has to steal a white man's boat to get his impregnated Lulu to a doctor because of her contractions during a life threatening flood disaster facing the community. Another African American male's life is put at risk because of a female, in this case an African American one, and the female's natural birth-giving process is a causal factor that results in the death of both characters. Mann is killed for stealing the boat, and Lulu dies because of the lack of medical attention that whites refuse to give her at the time.

The female character, regardless of race, continues to be the initiator of the action in both short fiction and novels. A white female inadvertently stumbles upon Big Boy and his buddies sunning nakedly in the short story "Big Boy Leaves Home." Though the young males have crossed the racial boundaries by trespassing on the property belonging to a white male, another white female, like Mary Dalton, initiates the violent reaction of the white patriarchy toward these young African American boys. Even when Wright began to write his existential novel, *The Outsider,* there had to be a rationale for Cross Damon's disgust with and departure from reality as he finds himself entrapped between marriage and adultery. Cross Damon's wife, Dot, characterized as the nagging shrew, along with his impregnated girlfriend and chastising mother, provides Wright's male protagonist with the background for his existential escape. Wright uses a series of female oppressors in the novel as the major cause for Cross Damon's existential sojourn, what could be called his male escape, and Fetterley's analysis of Irving's "Rip Van Winkle" *provides* a conceptual frame for analyzing this aspect of Wright's novel. The women are primarily characterized as shrews, and Cross Damon escapes by joining his male companions and by leaving for New York City.

Also, in "Long Black Song," the sexual act that occurs between Sarah, an African American female, and the white traveling salesman, is the epitome of female exploitation for narrative action. When the white salesman lures Sarah into sleeping with him, notwithstanding the attraction they both have for each other, Wright is presenting to the reader the societal taboo, the forbidding of sexual relations between whites and African Americans in early southern America. Again, we encounter a female who provides the "Wright stuff to put the African American male at risk. Like Mann in

"Down by the Riverside," Sarah's husband, Silas, eventually loses his life because of her actions. When he discovers that an illicit sex act has occurred, his retaliation sparks a vehement reaction from the white patriarchy. This "Wright stuff" gives credence to the argument that Wright's female characters are used to not only help Wright achieve his artistic objectives, but they illumine male problems to such an extent that they, according to the strategy of the storyteller, warrant discard. The common interpretation of viewing Wright as sexually exploiting the female is one thing, but beyond that is Wright's consistency in using females to set the narrative wheels in motion for the ensuing action and climax. As the examples from some of Wright's major fiction have suggested, the narrative conflict is continuously woven from some event or action involving a female; she is a necessary agent and a casual factor, creating the conflicts in male affairs, which become a priority in the situations of African American protagonists who are pitted against the antagonistic forces of a white patriarchy.

Once the female is introduced, the dynamics of her relations with males further reiterates her status as server of phallocentric interests and her use. For example, Bessie is accessible to satisfy Bigger's emotional and, of course, sexual needs. She has assisted with the feigned kidnapping and ransom note involving the murdered Mary Dalton; therefore, against her will, she becomes, according to Bigger, a needed accessory. Bessie is also aware of Bigger's risks: he has killed a white female, the most heinous crime that an African American man can commit in a racially divided American society. Both realize the heavy price that is on his head. Not only does Bessie, the girlfriend, become Bigger's only friend, but she also becomes "baggage" that must be disposed of if he wants to rid himself of all possibility of incrimination.

But regardless of her use, woman is ultimately outside of the community that Wright presents in his fiction. This exclusionary status is a consequence of the privileges afforded male characters that are agents and enforcers of male authority. Fetterley's interpretation of "Rip Van Winkle" keenly distinguishes male culture as the context from which nature and civilization derive their significance, and she views the female character, Dame Van Winkle, as a *persona non grata*. She states, "Where in this story is the female reader to locate herself? Certainly she is not Rip, for the fantasy he embodies is thoroughly male and is defined precisely by its opposition to woman" (9).

The conceptual frame that Fetterley formulates is one that entails the repudiation of woman after she has dutifully fulfilled her domestic role, not just for her male spouse but also for male authority—the patriarchy—from which her spouse's power is derived. Dame Van Winkle's service becomes inconsequential not just in the functions of the male world but on a more personal level in her relations with her spouse. Thus, Rip Van Winkle abandons his wife and goes off into the forest, a romantic and feminine symbol. Taking care of responsibilities is a masculine requirement and contributes to a masculine image. However, Rip's refusal to do so feminizes him, leaving those responsibilities to his wife. A reversal of roles occurs, according to Fetterley, for in addition to Dame Van Winkle's exclusionary status, "she is made a masculine authority figure and damned for it while qualities which are potentially admirable aspects of the female role are assigned to Rip and made positive because they are part of his character" (10). In other words, it is Rip's story and not Dame Van Winkle's.

Similarly, Bessie is the female companion who provides Bigger with moral and even economic support (stealing from the people she works for at his request); in essence, she could be viewed as nurturing, and, thus, her role as an African American domestic is appropriate. Yet Bigger rapes her, wielding his phallic power to assuage his anger, frustration, and fear. Subsequently, Bigger's most obvious motive for killing Bessie is the risk she poses for his capture. What France has suggested as the objectification of the female, i.e., her reduction" to the status of property," results in Bessie's repudiation and death. Such reductionism in *Native Son* conveys what France has also termed as "this negative polarity of the text."

If one views Bessie as symbolic of the mother and a nurturing figure, one may find that Bigger's need to escape from her and his compulsion to kill are the result of multiple inner conflicts. Nancy Chodorow's feminist-oriented psychoanalytical and sociological study, *The Reproduction of Mothering,* includes an analysis of mothers and their relationships with their sons that is very relevant to the nurturing factor in Wright's fiction and Bigger's particular case. Chodorow refers to Grete Bibring's[4] argument that "the decline of the husband's presence in the home has resulted in a wife as much in need of a husband as the son is of a father. This wife is likely to turn her affection and interest to the next obvious male—her son—and to become particularly seductive toward him" (qtd. in Chodorow 104). Chodorow's analysis also reveals that this type of relationship in male-dominated societies causes separation and individuation in a boy's life. She further concludes that this could eventually engender problems with the male son, resulting in a conflicting sense of gender and in "the castration of first his mother and then women in general" (107). Such castration takes place in *Native Son*, first, with Bigger's mother, who feels so victimized by his irresponsibility (hanging out with a gang and not seriously looking for work) that she states bitterly, "sometimes I wonder why I birthed you" (8). Mary becomes Bigger's second victim, who is decapitated so that her body will fit into an incendiary oven for cremating. Then there is Bessie, his third, whose head is smashed with a brick and whose body, still possessing life, is brutally disposed of. Clearly the female bears the brunt of this young man's involuntary and voluntary actions that deprive her of the right to live. They have been disposed of in the narrative; they must be because they have provided the narrative with its most poignant drama and their sacrifice is necessary so that Wright can proceed with Bigger's story—his flight from and eventual fight with white male authority.

If one follows up on Nagueyalti Warren's suggestion—to reveal Wright's motivation for his characterizations of females—one will find that Chodorow's theories resulting from her study of mother and son relationships are also appropriate for examining Wright's autobiographical *Black Boy*, with its familial situation of the absent father and its raw disclosures of the male self, especially in relation to the female Other. In her section "Preoedipal Mother-Son Relationships: the Clinical Picture," Chodorow contends that with the prolonged absence of the male comes a very strong emotional investment in the female, and "he projects his own fears and desires onto his mother, whose behavior he then gives that much more significance and weight" (105). Young Richard's caustic portrayal of his father, who abandons the family in Memphis for another woman, and the conflicting mother/son interactions throughout *Black Boy*, illustrate Chodorow's concepts regarding the mother/son relationship and the absent father. There is no doubt the suggestion of misogyny, not only because of a dysfunctional familial situation but also because the family has to function within the boundaries of a white (and) male-dominated society. According to Chodorow, because of the emotional investiture of the mother with the son, the mother acquires a phallic dimension. Conflicts, therefore, make the male feel castrated and he, in turn, as noted earlier, castrates the mother.

This rejection and discard, as well as reversal of roles, are also demonstrated in another Wright short story, "Fire and Cloud." The protagonist, Reverend Taylor, has emerged as a leader of the black church and community but is endangered for collaborating with members of the communist party who wish to help him fight the injustices whites pose regarding the hunger and joblessness facing the African American community. Reverend Taylor demands that his wife, May ("May I"), take on the following responsibility regarding a meeting he must have with all the key agents (males) in a strategic plan to ease the suffering of his people: keep the white mayor (whom he fears) at bay, go to the basement of the church and tell the deacons he is with the mayor and wait, and then tell the Reds (Hadley and Green) to come through a room and clandestinely meet with him before he faces the others. Preceding this intricate operation in the narrative are several violent confrontations that Reverend Taylor has had with white males, who have left him powerless and socially impotent, even with his own people. The reader then observes the obedient, subservient May receiving these directions, successfully executing them, only to be "immasculated" by her mate. Reverend Taylor responds to May's concerned queries with, "Don't bother me now May! . . . Naw May! Now please! Yuh worrin me!" (379) and "Do what I tell yuh, May?" (366).

May successfully executes Reverend Taylor's plan, but like Dame Van Winkle, she becomes an unappreciated servant, in fact a nagging shrew. And Bigger's response to Bessie when she questions his ransom note plan is "You going to do what I say" (179)! Thus, the reader observes that the female achieves parity with the male when her assistance is needed to execute or resolve conflicts, but she becomes victimized because of the phallocentric dynamics of male culture, which alienate the female, put her back in her place, and remind her that she is no longer a valued agent in what is deemed as "male affairs."

In *Black Boy* this dialectic of acceptance and need paired with repudiation and discard is observed when the reader is introduced to Mrs. Moss, the landlady on Beale Street whom Wright encounters when he arrives in Memphis after leaving Mississippi. After his initial meeting with Mrs. Moss and her daughter, Bessie, Wright amazingly declared, "It was on reputedly disreputable Beale Street in Memphis that I had met the warmest, friendliest person I have ever known, that I discovered that all human beings were not mean and driving, were not bigots like other members of my family" (247). Yet after interacting with them and realizing that both mother and daughter saw him as a good prospect for marriage, Richard becomes awed and then annoyed at their eagerness. And when Bessie and Richard engage in conversation about her weaknesses in school, Bessie finally says, "Love is the most important thing," to which Richard responds, "I wondered if she were demented." Finally, Richard admits, "the behavior of the mother and daughter ran counter to all I had ever seen and known" (251).

For the first time, Wight has encountered females that admired him—his intelligence, good looks, and manners. It was a situation so alien to a young boy whose mother, grandmother, and aunts were as oppressive as the whites he was escaping from in Mississippi; his labeling them "bigots" attests to his equating them with threatening southern whites. Moreover, the authoritarian position they held in his life created a masculine disposition that made most confrontations with them become just as threatening as those incidents provoked by Jim Crow practitioners. And though Mrs. Moss and Bess are crucial to his survival upon his arrival in Memphis, he is simply annoyed and repulsed by their pursuits to make him a husband and son in-law. They, too, are repudiated.

In addition, Wright's artistic vision does not include the female as a leader of or deliverer for her people, regardless of her positive imaging at the outset of the narrative. He assigns most of his African American male characters such qualities as courage, stamina, and determination, and even if these qualities are attributed to the female, she never prevails. Something bad always happens to her; she is expendable. Aunt Sue in "Bright and Morning Star" (*UTC*) exists as a vital yet expendable entity as she undauntedly fights the system to protect her son, Johnny-Boy, who has been betrayed by the feigned white communist, Booker. But Aunt Sue pays a very high price for her courage—an old woman unmercifully beaten and then shot by her enemies. Thus, regardless of the stature Aunt Sue achieves in the narrative, she cannot prevail, despite her age and, especially, her gender. She, too, must be disposed of. All of Wright's characters are limited in their right to live and even die peaceably, and the female, regardless of her use, has a lesser chance of achieving her life's goals in comparison to her counterpart. And even though few of Wright's male figures literally prevail positively (Big Boy and Fishbelly are an exception), such as Bigger, their dominance in relation to female characters exists until their end. Wright's males become tragic heroes who basically provoke a sympathetic reading. However, Wright's females are diminished characters and when not so, like Aunt Sue, they still are not spared; they are subjugated not only to the African American male but also to the wider social constructs affecting race, class, and gender.

But there is occasionally a shift occurring in Wright's characterizations of females when they are mulatto or white as in the case of Gloria, the mulatto in *The Long Dream*, and Eva Blount, the "white" female communist in *The Outsider*. Gloria is a vital agent for the exposure of the white police chief, Cantley, because of her co-conspiratorial status in protecting Fishbelly (the protagonist in (*The Long Dream*) and his father, the notorious Tyree Tucker. She assists in hiding the cancelled checks that constitute evidence of payoffs and bribes involving the illegal activities of businesses in the Bottom owned by Tyree, a successful mortician, and a Dr. Bruce. After Gloria has assisted in hiding the evidence that is needed to incriminate Cantley, Tyree's son, Fishbelly, comes to retrieve them. When Gloria is persuaded to relinquish the cancelled checks and is convinced that Tyree will avoid trouble, she admonishingly gives Fishbelly advice and counsel. However, Fishbelly's response is keenly different from Bigger's to Bessie and Reverend Taylor's to May. He thinks, "Her intelligence, her whiteness, her flawless manner of enunciations made him endow her with the magical power and cruel cunning of the white world and he began to believe her. Maybe, his father, Tyree, ought to give up and flee . . . (276). For a moment, Gloria's whiteness is influential. Subsequently, when Fishbelly reports to his father that Gloria is upset and does not want to relinquish the checks, Tyree responds, "Yeah, I thought that . . . women can't understand these things" (276). The chauvinistic manner in which the men handle the conflict results in their ignoring Gloria's advice, much to the detriment of Tyree, who eventually loses his life.

Moreover, Gloria's solution to Tyree and Fishbelly's problems with the white power structure is not just woman's folly, for the cancelled checks, which Tyree clandestinely harbored, become the key evidence for disclosing payoffs and illegalities. This event becomes a major subplot in the novel, and despite the contribution Gloria makes, she is expendable. Her suggestions go unheeded, and she has to leave town and begin a new life. Fishbelly is almost influenced by her intelligence, but his father's phallogocentric mode of reasoning reminds him of his obligation to male authority. Even Gloria's whiteness and intelligence are inconsequential.

Eva Blount, the white female in *The Outsider*, acquires an even more exalted stature because she is irresistible to Cross Damon; he cannot resist her nor she him. As his communist comrade, she offers her friendship, support, and, most important, cautionary advice; however, Cross Damon's transgressions, i.e., his series of murders, make it difficult for her to love him unconditionally. Because of the conflict between her love for Cross and her knowledge of his murders, she commits suicide; Eva's leap from a window is Wright's strategy for ridding the narrative of a female character who has been so politically and amorously connected to his protagonist. However, because of Wright's artistic and philosophical compulsions with Cross, Eva, too, must be eliminated regardless of the positive impact she has had on him.

Margaret Walker Alexander's biography, *Richard Wright: Daemonic Genius*, overtly discusses what many critics have reluctantly expressed about Wright—his relationships and marriages to white women—and points to Wright's imaging of Eva's and Gloria's whiteness. Walker's Freudian-based analysis of Wright, the man and the artist, makes the assertion that Wright's "hatred of black women was complicated by inferiority feelings and self hatred" and that "he believed that black women were easy prey to white men, not loyal to their black men and capable only of a blind animal sexuality . . . the way he discussed and treated black women in his fiction" (163). It is this blind and "racialized sexuality" that JanMohamed attributes to Wright's portrayal of Bessie's and Bigger's relationship because it symbolically suggests the stereotypical views that, historically, some have had regarding the sexuality of African Americans––as animalistic and amoral. Since Bigger brutishly forces Bessie to copulate with him without her consent, which is in essence rape, the only rape in the novel, Wright has been accused of perpetuating or suggesting a predominately uncivilized and animalistic relationship that exists between African-American male and female lovers. Walker Alexander concludes that, based on his two marriages to white women and his fiction, Wright "demanded an ideal, perfect, and blameless mate, a woman on a pedestal, a goddess, and, therefore, in the mirror image of southern white culture, she had to be white, beautiful, intelligent, morally above reproach, and completely submissive to him" (163).

However, regardless of Wright's racialized intentions in addressing the race problems in America, the female remains subjugated and negated, and the African American male often is killed. Thus, neither survives, which contributes to the obvious pessimism and nihilism of Wright's fiction; however, the writer's intention is not to tell the female's story but to use, abuse, and discard her so that the forcefulness of narrative conflict and drama is absorbed by the male protagonist. One may wonder why the female character does not engender a more harmless exit from the narrative or that her causation for narrative conflict is less stinging or nonexistent. This seems to be the impetus for Margaret Walker Alexander's study of Wright—that this writer's uniqueness is because of the demonic nature of his artistic consciousness—formed by every aspect of a troubled childhood and challenging adulthood (a conflictual life) and the literature he absorbed.

In addition, Wright's treatment of the white female/African American male relationship presents a dialectic involving the interrelatedness of sex and racism—that racism is grounded in what Stephen Michael Best calls the black man's threat to white masculinity, which warrants "upholding the purity of southern white womanhood" (118-119). Wright also suggests this unconscious desire for the white woman, e.g., Bigger's gesture of desire for Mary before he accidentally smothers her in *Native Son*, Cross Damon's and Eva's mutual attraction in *The Outsider*, and Johnny-Boy's white girlfriend, Reva, in "Bright and Morning Star." Wright's fiction is certainly not oblivious to interracial relationships, and this is reflected in the choices he made in his own life. Nevertheless, he realized the risks the African-American male posed in such relationships, not only with the white community, but the African American one, as well. The historical phenomenon of lynching and oftentimes the ostracizing by the African American community at the very hint of an African American male having any association with a white woman confirm this risk.

One might also observe that Wright contrasts his characterization of the mulatto and fair-skinned female with that of dark-skinned Maybelle in *The Long Dream*. When Maybelle observes Fishbelly and his buddies choosing lighter-skinned women at the club, she begins to spew insults and retorts, "You goddamn white-struck fools just hungry for the meat the white man's done made in nigger town! Go on, you cheap niggers, and lap the white man's crumbs" (170). This "second voice" imbued in the narrative discourse points to Mikhail Bakhtin's notion of the "double-voiced discourse," a type of dialogism (324) which indicates Wright's deviation from the monolithic imaging of male/female relations, particularly, in this novel. And the intensity and vigor of Mabelle's speech relate directly to Bakhtin's theory of heteroglossia, which he defines as "another's speech in another's language, serving to express authorial intentions but in a refracted way." Such speech "expresses simultaneously two different intentions: the direct intention of the character who is speaking, and the refracted intention of the author" (324).

In addition to this heteroglossic stance in Wright created by Maybelle's speech are Wright's Marxist overtones and this text's ripeness for womanist concerns; he presents the class and, especially, color conflict, known as colorizing, that exists within the infrastructure of the African American community. Maybelle is aware of her station in life, particularly, as a result of color. When the lighter-skinned females are chosen by Fishbelly and his buddies, all African American men, Maybelle realizes the appeal and higher rank of the lighter-skinned black woman; thus, Wright uses Maybelle to combat this tendency of some African American males. A womanist interpretation of this scene is appropriate because it reveals the historical phenomenon of colorizing that Wright conveys; he is not only pitting the darker-skinned woman against the lighter-skinned one but also presenting woman as commodity. Both phenomena create further conflict and victimize both women. This is just one aspect of Wright's fiction that contributes to the complexity of his total treatment of the African American experience. Such treatment is like a prism, revealing the complexities of race, class, and gender issues, with each being equally profound. Though Wright's male consciousness pervades his fiction so powerfully, he makes some attempts to address the peculiarities and complexities of the African American female experience.

Another text that presents a complexity in characterizing the African American female is Wright's short story, "Long Black Song," noted earlier. The criticism primarily focuses on Wright's suggestion of "the bitch in heat," producing this whore-like effect in text and in film, with his portrayal of Sarah, a lone wife whose husband, Silas, has gone to town to sell his crop. A hot, simmering rural environment surrounding the young wife and young white salesman creates this primitive context for their meeting. Day has turned to darkness while the young white salesman has been trying to sell Sarah a gramophone, and after asking for a drink of water at the well, a physical encounter occurs: "His shoulder touched hers. In the darkness she felt his warm hands fumbling for the rope . . . . She extended the rope through the darkness. His fingers touched her breasts. 'Oh!' She said it in spite of herself. He would think she was thinking about that. And he was a white man. She was sorry she had said that" (337). Sarah's immediate thoughts of racial violation occur, yet the episode continues with what some have perceived as her suspicious resistance because Wright imbues her with such sensual traits—again this "the bitch in heat" effect. Yet, simultaneously, Wright has Sarah respond, "'Naw Mistah! . . . . But he's a *white* man. A *white* man . . . . Naw, naw . . . . Mistah, Ah cant do that'" (337). Regardless of how critics may interpret this scene, it points to the historical phenomenon of the rape and exploitation of the African and African American female during enslavement, for the white salesman takes sexual liberties with a rural African American woman who, regardless of resistance or submission, has no power, no choices. On the other hand, the nuance of consent is also suggested, creating this indeterminate aspect of the narrative that precludes any definite assessment of Wright's intention with this character. Nonetheless, she is necessary for the conflict she creates, and after her husband discovers her infidelity and is eventually killed by white males, the narrative ends with her "running into the hills," into oblivion. Her voice in the phallic-centered conflict of the text is in the form of causation only; she is the cause of Silas's combat with white males, his exhibition of militancy, for he is undaunted in expressing his anger and revenge for the white male's transgressions in his home. The finality of the narrative is woven to provoke a sympathetic reading of Silas's story, yet Sarah's sufferings are so mercurial because of the uncertainties surrounding her encounter, and even when she tries to articulate what happened, she is beaten like an animal by Silas before he takes on the final battle with white males.

Wright's complexity does not preclude his unequivocal demonstration of misogyny in "Long Black Song" and other texts, especially as African American females and males interact with each other under the constraints of a powerful white and male-dominated culture, often the root cause of such. *Lawd Today*, a lesser-known work initially entitled *Cesspool* and Wright's first complete novel, is such a text. Though *Lawd Today* featured a male protagonist and his personal and social conflicts, it is just as much about the abuse and ill treatment of a female, Lil, as it is about a day in the life of Jake Jackson, the central character. Most of the criticism treating *Lawd Today* emphasizes Wright's use of stark realism and modernism, as well as his rendering of the pathos of the African American male experience. Such critical reading views Lil's abuse as coincidental to Jake's chaotic life. This is the effect of the text, considering the sexism grounded in it and the dearth of female characters it and other Wright fiction have to positively influence the female reader regarding her own gender identity. Therefore, Fetterley's assertion concerning Irving's influence on the female reader certainly applies to Wright when she states, "the female reader is a divided self. She is asked to identify with Rip against herself, to be at once both repressor and repressed, and ultimately to realize that she is neither" (11). Irving's characters do not carry the historical baggage of enslavement as Wright's, and explicit in Wright's consistent and persistent focus on the African American male in his fiction is the prevailing image of his subject as the primary target of oppression.

As a result, the female character is subsumed in the African American male experience in Wright's fiction. Yet the female has played a major role in determining the dynamics of the male experience; after all, within her body, she brings the seed of life into fruition. She thus becomes the primary caretaker of life from its very beginning in all patriarchal cultures. As a result of such patriarchal agency in most cultures, females become subjugated and alienated from the main currents. Richard Wright admired western civilization to such an extent that his vision was blurred by it. Though he addresses a part of the American experience and tells his story, he was unable to transcend the boundaries of a patriarchal culture and configure a balanced imaging of femaleness in his total artistic vision. However, regardless of their fate, Wright recognizes how vital female characters are to his fiction and his artistic purpose. While they would have to be subjugated to Wright's male characters, he could not avoid positing them as necessary agents. Thus, the female character in the fiction of Richard Wright becomes a significant factor in his narrative formula for producing compelling and provocative drama, and it is this type of drama that created Wright's artistic identity and complexity in the tradition of American and, particularly, African-American literature.

NOTES

1   It is reported that Wright wanted to write a novel on women in American society and expressed a particular interest in the African American domestic. This quote comes from Wright's introductory essay, "How Bigger Thomas Was Born," which is included in *Native Son*, a restored text, published by The Library of America in 1998. All references to *Native Son* are from this edition.

2   Abdul JanMohamed's essay cites Michel Foucault's *The History of Sexuality, Volume I: An Introduction* as omitting the field in which "the deployment of sexuality intersects with race" (94), which JanMohamed identifies as "racialized sexuality." He presents a critique of Foucault's matrix and goes beyond it to present his own paradigm of racialized sexuality and its application to *Native Son*, particularly, differentiating the alleged rape and actual murder of May and the actual rape and murder of Bessie.

3   Barbara Smith, Alice Walker, and Bell Cook represent a cadre of African American feminist and womanist (Walker, especially) theorists who recognized the need for an alternative approach to addressing the issues and challenges involving the woman of color in patriarchal and American societies.

4   Chodorow utilizes Grete Bibring's research on the negative reactions of male sons toward their mothers in single parent families with absent fathers.

CHAPTER 2

Male Bonding/Homosocialism

It is ironical that females have such a germane role, given this male-centeredness in Wright's fiction. Since they are the stimulus for the dynamics of male experience, particularly narrative conflict, their use continues with Wright's representation of male groups, e.g., male bonding, which occurs in both short fiction and novels. One theorist who treats this concept in American novels is Donald J. Greiner, whose *Women Enter the Wilderness: Male bonding and the American Novel of the 1980s*, contrasts male bonding in 1980s novels with canonized American fiction in which the bonding of males warrants the abandonment of the female. Thus, Greiner's observation of abandonment of or escape from femaleness, which he also views as a tradition of nineteenth century fiction as well, parallels Judith Fetterley's assessment of Washington Irving's "Rip Van Winkle." Though Greiner asserts that this abandonment wanes in the 1980s novels by white males—that men enter the wilderness but carry their women with them—he nevertheless presents an appropriate analysis of male bonding in traditional American fictional texts. Greiner formulates two basic and perhaps obvious premises under girding male bonding in such texts: male bonding encourages criticism of women and male bonding empowers masculinity, especially in terms of physical and intellectual prowess.

This concept of female abandonment has as its predecessor the observations of Leslie Fieldler, who cites "this strategy of evasion" in American classics, most of which, except for Nathaniel Hawthorne's *Scarlet Letter*, have male protagonists. According to Fieldler, it is "this retreat to nature and childhood which makes our literature (and life!) so charmingly and infuriatingly "boyish" (xxi). This "boyish" retreat develops into a fraternal experience with other males or a form of male companionship as Griener and Fieldler both observe in James Fennimore Cooper's *The Last of the Mohicans* (xxi).

Richard Wright and other canonized African-American novelists are certainly not immune to this tradition of male bonding that Greiner and Fieldler have observed. Wright is not, especially, because he is so strongly influenced by both canonized American and European male writers whose fiction reflects the trends of traditional patriarchal societies where male bonding is so elemental. However, regardless of the male aggregate, the necessity of the female is still relevant in Wright's fiction, for in several of his texts females engender male bonding because of an unsolicited "intrusion" in male affairs. This intrusion reveals itself in several roles: as nagging mothers and girl friends (the shrew), as incriminating white girls, and as challengers to the normalcy of black male agency in a white patriarchal culture.

As gender and feminist criticism gained momentum in the twentieth century, the terminology and conceptualization used to articulate its ideology changed or complemented traditional thinking. Eve Sedgwick's *Between Men: English Literature and Male Homosocial Desire* is one critical text that explores the varied forms of what has been initially termed male bonding, or what Sedgwick specifically labels, *male homosocialism*,[1] which includes male homosocial desire, homoeroticism, and homosexuality. Thus, the bonding of males or females is termed "homosocialism," and according to Sedgwick, "'homosocialism' is a word occasionally used in history and the social sciences, where it describes social bonds between persons of the same sex; it is a neologism, obviously formed by analogy with homosexual, and just as obviously meant to be distinguished from 'homosexual.' In fact, it is applied to such activities as 'male bonding,' which may, as in our society, be characterized by intense homophobia, fear, and hatred of 'homosexuality'" (1).

With males as major characters in Wright's fiction, their bonding empowers them regardless of the maltreatment they receive from whites and the challenges that women pose; their bonding is used as a coping mechanism that responds to white oppression and gender challenges. Male bonding or male homosocialism also functions as a combatant force that captures and recaptures the strength that African American males need to affirm a masculine identity in a society that historically and consistently has threatened and challenged black masculinity in the context of both race and gender. However, since females are largely victimized in male dominated societies, male bonding becomes either an overt or a covert way of flaunting existing power and reiterating control. Thus, one understands Greiner's observation of how male bonding engenders negative representations of females and Fiedler's critique of traditional American writers who "shy away from permitting in their fiction the presence of full-fledged, mature women, giving us instead monsters of virtue or bitchery, symbols of rejection or fear of sexuality" (xix).

The historical phenomenon of victimization of females and African American males invokes gender and racialized discourses among Wright's males. In Wright's fiction, as in real life, there is not only the racialized victimization of males but also females; however, this writer creates situations and scenarios to portray the latter as being just as oppressive as their male white counterparts. Thus, most females become targets of criticism or physical or verbal abuse, as targets of male rage, or, as Fiedler has suggested, "jocularity" (xxii). This jocularity (a lesser form of victimization but nonetheless a serious one) occurs in one of Wright's stories, "Big Boy Leaves Home," where criticism or simply "poking fun" of females or femaleness occurs in the form of signifying, a speech act that Henry Louis Gates coins as trope in the African American vernacular; Wright's characters use signifying to target both females and whites. Often, concomitant with the signifying, which is also an exhibition of cognitive skills, is a physical challenge that occurs within the group. Both operatives, the signifying and the exhibition of physical prowess, are strategies of empowerment that Wright's males use for coping with what he has reduced to the two adversaries in an African American male's life: females, both African American and white and, of course, white males.

Wright's brief career as a postal worker had a significant impact on his fiction and nonfiction. He uses the postal worker(s) not only as individual character(s) but also as a male group; *Lawd Today* and *The Outsider* are major fictional texts of such import. Interestingly, in *Lawd Today* Wright focuses primarily on a 24 hour slice of Jake Jackson's life as a postal employee, yet his subtext is the oppression, castigation, and exploitation of females. Arnold Rampersad's comments on the publishing history of Wright's *Lawd Today* reveal that "the novel made the rounds of the major commercial publishers without success or encouragement until after his death" (2); Rampersad speculates that publishers may have been "repulsed by the extreme realism in the novel, as well as the raucous language and sexual obsession on the part of Jake and *his buddies*" (2). The verbal and physical abuse of Lil, Jake's wife, causes her to become a passive female, as well as the catalyst for Jake's escape from home to the comfort of his buddies, the barber shop, his job at the post office, and his night out on the town; Lil is the catalyst for his escape, and practically each scenario of male bonding is accompanied by a continuum of signifying that characterizes females as "conquered bitches." As a result, *Lawd Today* becomes one of Wright's representative texts because of male bonding or male homosocialism, which provides the context for gender and racial banter.

This analysis of Wright's representation of gender will examine the dynamics of male bonding/homosocialism as a narrative technique that either overtly or covertly implicates the female in three selected texts: the short story "Big Boy Leaves Home (the first story in *Uncle Tom's Children* (1938); the posthumously published novella, *Rite of Passage* (1993), and Wright's existential novel, *The Outsider* (1953). Though the individuated male protagonist prevails and persists in Wright's fiction, male groups manage to distinguish and, especially, empower themselves. Of course, racism is a primary target; however, in addition, one observes the use of the female character as a catalyst for racialized narrative conflicts and male escape.

"Yo Mama don't Wear No Drawers" is the first line of Wright's "Big Boy Leaves Home." Historically and culturally labeled as "playing the dozens,"

Wright's use of this folk idiom sets the playful and carefree tone and texture of the narrative's beginning. Gates' discourse on signifying is appropriate for examining the dozens as not only an African American cultural entity but one that implicates gender as well. According to Gates, the dozens is one among many "black rhetorical tropes", which include "masking, loud talking, specifying, testifying, calling out of one's name, sounding, rapping, and playing the dozens" (286); its implications of gender, both male and female are important. One might ask, "Why Yo Mama Don't Wear No Drawers'?" Why Not, "Yo Papa Don't Wear No Drawers." The answer lies in the realization of how male power is demonstrated in African American culture; playing the dozens and many acts of signifying primarily engage males yet often focus on females. It is usually a male exhibition, i.e., considered "a male thing" although females can participate. Big Sweet in Zora Neale Hurston's *Dust Tracks* is an example of a signifying priestess. Nevertheless, playing the dozens is intended to insult, undermine, cajole, and humorize; it is simply not generally viewed as a female verbal enterprise, but, most important, it often focuses on the female. Wright's use of the dozens reveals the continuance of a long African American tradition that has become inherited and demonstrated by such contemporaries as Arsenio Hall, Eddie Murphy, and Will Smith. In fact, entertainer Oscar Brown, Jr. is most noted for his version of the Signifying Monkey, a folk parody on the interplay between animal characters, with the monkey as trickster and instigator—the signifier.

However, regardless of how the reader interprets this introductory scenario in the narrative, the camaraderie, the laughter, the warmth of the sun, and the union of four boys with the natural environment—Wright's pastoral and naturalist influences—present the innocence of Big Boy and his friends, Buck, Bobo, and Lester. And regardless of their being trespassers on the property of Ol Man Harvey, a white male, they belong to themselves and the communion of their union is ritualistically confirmed by a possession of their own—their folk culture, the dozens, which is unequivocally theirs. This aura of innocence and communion is often cited by critics, but it is immediately contrasted with the evil of white racism and violence awaiting its young victims.

A critique of "Big Boy Leaves Home" by Hal Blythe and Charlie Sweet presents a list of those studies that focus on the violence of the narrative in contrast to the idyllic moment Wright captures with his characters and setting. In addition, Blythe and Sweet employ a psychosexual approach, citing the narrative's female and sexual symbolism and its "suspended sexuality"; they make reference to Wright's covert treatment of female sexuality. According to these critics, the opening line, "Yo mama don wear no drawers," suggests "the unconscious awareness that the mother also possesses a sexual nature" (31). But it also suggests a mocking and ridiculing of the female, as well. The following line, "Ah seen a when she pulled em off" (239)[2] is one that indicates a disrobing of the female and exposing of her body. The male has had the opportunity to see to it, for "Ah seena" suggests not only the male's witness to the act but his possession of a private knowledge, like that of the voyeur who uses it as a weapon of disclosure and embarrassment. The closing of the line, "When she pulled em off," immediately exposes the female's sexual area, reiterating and confirming exposure and the power of the male's knowledge. Intermittent with this trope is Wright's inclusion of the boy's joyous and celebrative behavior; he describes them as: "Another, shrill, cracking" and "adolescent" (239). He also reports them "laughing easily" as they threw themselves on the grass (239). The entire trope unfolds with female mockery as its aim. The female is a significant agent for provoking this signifying ritual in African American folklore.

Big Boy's name suggests man-child, of course, and the events in the story demonstrate the leadership role he assumes with the group. He provides the group with a repertoire of words to complete the trope, suggesting to them a last line that further mocks the female. They realize they have to stop with the *line*, "N she hung 'em out in the hall . . ." (239). They express the desire to go further, "Ah wished Ah knowed some mo lines t tha song," and when they ask "what goes wid hall," it is Big Boy who supplies the word, "quall," thus sending his buddies into a laughing frenzy. They acknowledge his ability to not only supersede them in vocabulary but also humor. He reiterates his ingenuity by repeating the line, "N then she put em back on her Quall" (240)! Of course, "her quall" is Big Boy's signifying of the female's private parts—her womanhood or "the body of woman," which becomes a refrain in *The Outsider*.

Big Boy's capsulation of the signifying trope is important in establishing not only the female as a focal point but also his leadership ability. After a series of playful melee, he exclaims to his male companions, "Ah mah smart nigger . . . thrusting out his chest" (245). However, as the narrative continues to unfold, the focus solely on the female in song wanes, and it shifts to the male, with both sexes as the target to ridicule:

> LAS ONE INS A OLD DEAD DOG
> THAS YO MA!
> THAS YO PA!
> THAS BOTH YO MA N YO PA! (246)

The male subject, however, only capsulates a chant that has essentially marked and mocked the female for signifying purposes.

After they have bonded in song and signifying at the beginning of the narrative, the young boys bond with mother earth. The lay themselves against the warm earth that feels "jus lika bed" (240), experiencing a moment of ecstasy and fetality, of being safe and secure in mother earth's womb, like the female womb that encloses fragile life so securely. Again, this idyllic moment is reiterated with such phrases as, "Jesus, Ah could stay here forever, Ah kin feel tha ol sun going all thu me," and finally, "Feels like mah bones is warm" (240). Though the female has been the object of mockery at the beginning of the narrative, it is mother earth, *la femme*, that gives them warmth and comfort.

Following this moment is the intrusion of a whistle—the real world—signaling the coming of a train, a phallic intrusion, what Blythe and Sweet refer to as "an objective correlative for their (the young boys) emerging sexual power" (16). In addition, the train becomes a stimulant for another folk singing and bonding activity; it sparks the reminiscence of a spiritual chant, "Dis train bound for Glory," followed by the response, "Gee, thas a good ole song!" (241). Yes, "Dis Train" is "a good ole song" because these young boys are reminded of the train as the means by which African Americans are carried away from the racial tensions of the South to what many envisioned at that time, the 1930s, as the opportunities of the north. The song also creates the solidarity that is needed to give them the resilience to combat and endure the threatening laws and tactics of white southerners. Moreover, Wright puts into the mouth of Big Boy an ideal of the African American community—"They say colored folks up Noth is got ekual rights" (248). Therefore, the dozens, the chants, and simply things done in unison represent Wright's way of using the folk medium as a solidifying agent for black male homosocialism in which convening and bonding become a coping strategy for both racial and gender issues.

Along with this cultural phenomenon that brings about such homosocialism is the male tactic that involves a display of strength and power. Big Boy has made several gestures to insure his reign of masculine power, which entails his ability to outwit and out think his comrades—this intellectual prowess and ability to demonstrate his physical strength: he has supplied the group with the rhyming word to complete the dozens song; he has played trickster by his gaseous emission (i.e., breaking wind and then feigning sleep, causing the others to become disgusted and victimized); and he has finally proved himself the strongest when they try to wrestle him down, but to no avail. Whether it is a display of verbal skills or a physical match, in order to reign as leader, Wright's male characters must excel verbally and physically; this is especially the case with Bigger and his buddies in *Native Son*, Jake and his buddies in *Lawd Today*, and Cross Damon in *The Outsider*.

Wright, consequently, takes the narrative to another level, a level that renders his artistic purpose—to address the problem of racism in America, especially regarding the African American male. Wright engages the female, again, as a pivotal agent for plot development or as a target of male frustration and scorn. It is not enough for Big Boy and his buddies to commit their transgressions with truancy (skipping school that day) and trespassing on Ol Man Harvey's property; it is also characteristic of Wright to use the white woman as a disruptive agent as her appearance becomes intrusive in relation to the introductory setting and tone of the narrative. After Wright has depicted one perfect moment in these young African American boys' lives, white Bertha, like Mary Dalton in *Native Son*, the white female decoy in *The Long Dream*, and even Eva in *The Outsider*, appears and causes their worlds to become topsy turvy. The white woman, thus, is a catalyst for Wright's narrative conflict.

The racialized gender conflict, Michael Best's idea of lynch law, is also presented in Wright's other short fiction and novels as in "Big Boy Leaves Home." However, according to the paradigm that Best develops with Wright's *Black Boy*, "Lynch Law is, from Dick's (Wright's) narrative perspective, radically indeterminate" (119). It can take on so many forms, with the instigators, in this case whites, having limitless control and power. Big Boy prevails, but not unequivocally, for the threat of lynch law remains to continuously victimize him and his buddies; even the entire African American community suffers racial violence because of the transgressions of Big Boy and his friends. Black male transgressive behavior is dealt with via lynch law, and as Best suggests, racial injustice takes on many other variations of denial and violence. And Wright's use of signifying in the context of black male agency is a combative and even flirtatious response to the reality of risks surrounding the lives of African American males.

This intermingling of sex and racism is prevalent in Wright's fiction, especially, when the white female character is cast as instigator or cataclysmic threat. She, too, is subjugated to the white patriarchy and is, of course, bait to effect the African American male's demise. Moreover, she is often viewed as the white male's most strategic weapon for victimizing African American males; this intermingling of sex and race in Wright's fiction is a familiar approach in which he utilizes the historical phenomenon of racialized (black/white) sexuality, which Jan Mohammed explores in *Native Son*. Even though Bertha stumbles upon the naked young adolescents, she undoubtedly has left her mate because she is alone when she encounters them. Subsequently, she is compelled to alert Jim, who is her finance' (the protector of "the angel in the house") and Ol Man Harvey's son. Also Jim's military uniform and rifle could be interpreted as militaristic and phallocentric symbols of black male oppression and white male authority, like the armed policeman in urban America, whether white or African American, male or female. Regardless, when Big Boy jumps on Jim, taking his rifle, firing it and killing him, after he has killed his friends, Buck and Lester, the transference of power and the impotency of the white male are concretized. Big Boy takes control and exhibits power, which, for African American males, has historically and systematically been subdued, thwarted, and penalized.

Finally, as the conflict begins to resolve, the first person Big Boy runs to for refuge is, of course, his mother, who envelops him like mother earth. "Ma," in turn, calls for daughter, Lucy, who eventually summons the father. Mothers and females are often used as primary seats of refuge after those "phallic-status" conflicts occur. Dave Saunders goes straight to his mother, first, for permission to buy a pistol and, second, after accidentally killing Jenny the mule in "Almos a Man"; Bigger returns home, as well as to Bessie after he has killed Mary in *Native Son*; Wright himself runs to his mother on several occasions after troubling encounters with young white and African American boys in *Black Boy*; and little Johnny in *Rite of Passage* is first informed about his new foster parents by his present foster mother and sister. Thus, the female's necessity is again confirmed: phallic-centered conflicts are brought to her, she acts as intervening agent, and even though she is often imaged as annoyer and shrew, she is nonetheless the seat of comfort for African American male transgressors or innocent victims of conflict.

On the other hand, the marginalizing of the father figure, resulting in cameo appearances in some of Wright's narratives (an exception would be Tyree Tucker in *The Long Dream*) is hardly a mystery, for the absent father figure in Wright's fiction is a reflection of the absence of Wright's own father, who deserted the family in Memphis; Wright treats this abandonment in his autobiographical *Black Boy*. Moreover, females always surrounded Wright during his boyhood: his mother, his aunts, and his maternal grandmother. Female participation as mediator and comforter is, in Wright's world, germane to male affairs. And because of the varied roles, of nurturer, domesticator, and facilitator with family that African American females have played in their families throughout history, it is just as appropriate for the male to seek refuge with the female than with the male. Nancy Chodorow's theory concerning the absent father figure implicates the male as target for not only male anger but comfort, too.

However, in the context of the African American experience, the question that arises is why choose a female instead of a male (even when he is accessible), whose masculine agency as protector has been defined and demonstrated by the larger society. Perhaps since the African American male experiences unparalleled conflict in a racially divided male-dominated society—where white male rule is the norm—another African American male's position of authority is deemed impotent and powerless, especially when white males have originated the conflict. The black preacher, who may have autonomy in his community, is sometimes an exception, such as Reverend Mays, who, in "Fire and Cloud," is led to believe that his leadership is respected, only to find himself threatened and beaten by white vigilantism. Nevertheless, the African American female becomes the next agent of protection, warmth, and security, i.e., symbolizing the womb. Big Boy runs home to Ma, as do most of Wright's males, for she, as Wright has clearly demonstrated, is necessary for dealing with the crises of her wounded offspring and mate; Aunt Sue in "Bright and Morning Star," who comes to the aid of Johnny-Boy, and certainly Bessie, who comes to the aid of Bigger, clearly illustrate this pattern.

In the aforementioned context, one realizes the varied approaches Wright uses to either acknowledge the phenomenon of the absent father or to present the varied circumstances for it, e.g., a preexisting death, such as the case with Bigger's father in *Native Son* or the little boy in *Savage Holiday*. Regardless, his fiction presents both tenets of black male agency in the context of family and fatherhood; there are times when he is briefly present as in Wright's own case, where Wright eventually becomes a product of an absent father home. Thus, Wright was well-versed in the historical patterns of race and gender regarding family and the plight of African American males in American society. The history of black masculinity and the realities and mythologies issuing from the subject is rather definitively addressed in the series of essays edited by Ernestine Jenkins and Darlene Clark Hine. *A Question of Manhood, Volume II*, provides the historical context for understanding the factors surrounding black patriarchal concerns. According to one essayist, Robyn Wiegman,[3] the work of the Freedmen's Bureau to establish the newly freed slave as head of household was met with the following oppositional logic:

> The loss of one patriarchal organization of social life––
> that of slavery––and its replacement by the seeming

> egalitarianism of a male-dominated black family, then,
> has the effect of broadening the competitive dimensions
> of interracial masculine relations, especially as the black
> male's new property governance of black women threatens
> to extend to women of the dominant group as well.
>
> (Hine and Jenkins 358)

Thus, according to Wiegman, African American males as head of household were regarded as a patriarchal threat and competitor for the commodious female, both black and white. As suggested earlier, Wright does not exhibit a monolithic perspective on the father/husband figure; he can be present, as in the family of Big Boy and Fishbelly, or absent, as in that of Bigger and Cross, the latter making a conscious decision to desert his own family, as Wright's father did.

Another text that deals with the plight of young boys and, simultaneously, treats their bonding and homosocialism is Wright's most recently discovered novella, *Rite of Passage*. It is reported that the narrative reflects Wright's keen interest in adolescent gang culture as a result of his work with Chicago's Southside Boy's Club and the staff of New York state's Wiltwyck School for Boys—the same institution that becomes the home of another author, Claude Brown, who reminisces about his own engagement with gangs in the autobiographical *Manchild in the Promised Land*.[4] Wright begins *Rite of Passage* with Johnny Gibbs as he does "Big Boy Leaves Home" with Big Boy. Both begin the day with such splendor: Big Boy begins his day skipping school and swimming in the hole with his buddies, and Johnny has had a successful day at school after receiving a report card of all As, which is not surprising for Wright's characterization of this model student. However, ensuing events present change, what Gates has termed "Wright's overall aesthetic, based in . . . an agency of contrast" (qtd. in Best 116). When Johnny comes home from school, he finds that the parents whom he has always known are really foster parents and that the welfare office has declared he must leave this family and be adopted by other foster parents. As with Big Boy, females (mother and sister) must comfort him after informing him of such bad news. They try to help him cope, but they are unsuccessful.

Just as some of Bigger Thomas's actions are considered instinctual in *Native Son*, Wright also attributes instinctual behavior to Johnny Gibbs, who is incapable of understanding the news he receives from his mother and sister. This young man has always thought that his family was his biological family, only to find out differently. Having to leave them is beyond his comprehension, and his response attests to this, for he thinks, "the mother he loved so deeply was now disavowing him, cutting him off, telling him that all his life had been a lie. It was too much; he felt that he was standing in midair and would fall at any moment" (17).

In addition, since Johnny is experiencing feelings of rejection, the only way to combat the source of his pain, the mother and sister, is to run from them. He responds, "If you make me leave, I'll run off" (8). He has to move away from females in order to cope, and Big Boy, who moves toward females for comfort, has to abandon them to avoid a lynching. In *Rite of Passage* as in much of Wright's fiction, females are acting out of a culture that victimizes their loved ones, not because of the choices they have had to make but often because of the institutions that have governed their lives; females must submit to those institutions and laws that are primarily promulgated by white male authority. Their behavior, like Johnny's sister and mother, is involuntarily guided and controlled. Along with Bertha in "Big Boy," Johnny's mother and sister are just as victimized by the white patriarchy as the black youths. Bertha is co-opted by sexual taboos and laws, based on white male fears that have been instilled in the white female, and because of this, she involuntarily reacts to the sight of black male bodies sunning nakedly. The mother and daughter in *Rite of Passage* are victimized because they must adhere to the policy of the welfare office that is oppositional to all their efforts in providing Johnny with a stable, wholesome family life; Johnny's academic achievements and avoidance of gangs attest to these efforts. Michael Best's concept of lynch law and family law as the premise of early southern life is applicable, for the critic contends the following regarding the persona in *Black Boy*:

> From Dick's narrating perspective, family law is a
> heuristic tool of lynch law. That is to say, family law is
> the site where hegemony is made tangible, the domain
> where blacks give over their rights to agency . . . family
> law covers for a complicitous, conformist acquiescence in
> black communities caused by racism and segregation. (115)

But regardless of female complicity in dealing with male conflict, Wright must get back to his primary purpose—the plight of the African American male—and, thus, Johnny runs away and enters into male culture; it serves as refuge from a painful encounter with African American females, who play a crucial role in his escape, just like the female messengers from the welfare office who initially cause his dilemma. It is Johnny's initiation into the gang—his rite of passage—that also demonstrates how maleness defines and shapes itself, what Best terms "black male agency."

Since verbal wit, intellectual prowess, and physical strength are a prerequisite for acceptance in some male bonding and male homosocial situations, like Big Boy, Johnny, too, is embroiled in a series of challenges by his newly found friends—a gang led by an adolescent with a bald head, who has been named "Baldy" by his peers. Greiner notes that males have a more difficult time and that "since physical maturity is not enough for a male to be judged a man, the male must demonstrate by performance that he is worthy of bonding with males already initiated" (38). And Johnny does so in the cognitive, as well as affective realm.

Wright's dialogism involving the dynamics of male homosocialism points to this need for demonstrating intellectual superiority and outsmarting one's peers in wit. It is this type of exhibitionism that usually precedes any physical challenge. Baldy, the initial leader of the gang, has to eventually abdicate after Johnny has demonstrated his physical strength; however, Johnny's intellectualism precedes the physical challenge. Wright's chief males must warrant respect and achieve stature not because their superior wit is a valued element of the larger society but because it is respected in a familiar cultural realm, such as signifying. When this victory is signifying, e.g., Cross Damon with Joe and his buddies, Big Boy with his friends, and Bigger's dialogue with his buddies on the Blum robbery, this verbal wit contributes to the ascendancy of Wright's males in the ranks with their peers. Johnny proves himself intellectually at the outset, elevating himself in the eyes of the larger society but failing in the realm of street discourse and culture: "Goddamn, you're dumb...Maybe you're smart to the teachers in this school. But we can't use school shit" is Baldy's response (67). This statement parallels the response that Big Boy gets when he furnishes the gang with the word "quall" to rhyme with "hall," which becomes nonsensible to his other buddies, one of whom responds, "Man whoever hearda quall?" (239).

After Johnny's initial acceptance in the gang and after being labeled as "moocher," which in their terms is an orphan or runaway, he has to prove himself physically. He does so when he unknowingly provokes Baldy and subsequently defeats him. Baldy's defeat warrants abdication and Johnny ascends as gang leader, not simply because of his physical prowess but also because of an uncanny intelligence that the others feel may prove useful at some point in their relationship. Wright continuously endows his protagonists with qualities that set them apart from their peers. But their ascent to a higher rank with them does not occur without challenge; their leadership position must be earned. Big Boy's proclamation, "Ahma smart nigger," can also metaphorically mean "a Bad Nigger" as in the case with Bigger after his knife threat with Gus, and as in that of Cross Damon, who triumphantly teases his buddies and eventually ends up murdering one.

Moreover, after Johnny's physical strength has been determined, he must now complete his "rite of passage" by engaging in some type of criminal behavior. As stated earlier, in most male homosocial scenarios, males must be able to prove themselves in every aspect of the criteria that are used to determine their membership into male groups. Their bonding centers on sameness, and there is little if any room for difference or marked individuality. Baldy informs Johnny that as a runaway he must now learn how to mug and even murder, if necessary, to survive. Moreover, in male bonding situations Wright's males eventually get around to targeting white males; in some cases it is accidental and indirect, and in others it is intentional. Jim's and Bertha's appearance in "Big Boy" is coincidental to the young black males' truancy and trespassing. Blum is certainly the intended victim of Bigger and his buddies, and Johnny is instructed that he must mug a white male, the most sanctioned target of his frustration and anger.

> "Did you ever jump a black man?" Johnny asked.
> "Yes. White or black; they're all the same,"
> Badly said. "But I'd rather jump a white man,"
> Treetop said. "Yeah. Somehow it feels better,"
> Skinkie said. (104)

Wright has all of the events surrounding Johnny's rise to prominence in the gang and subsequent mugging lead to the vital female. *Rite of Passage* is an example of a cyclical technique in its inclusion of her. The narrative begins with females, with male experience at its center and ends with a female character, who is surprisingly and enigmatically introduced as a witness to the mugging. This character becomes a haunting image who yells, "You Boys!" Her presence is the most intriguing and lasting image for Johnny, who has thought that the mugging has gone unwitnessed. Yet the woman's phantom-like introduction in the narrative's ending becomes as intrusive and spontaneous as Bertha's sudden appearance and behavior in "Big Boy." The female in *Rite of Passage* becomes a silent burden that Johnny must now live with, especially since it seems as if the other gang members are unaware of her presence.

Wright endows his protagonist with such a sensibility to females that their existence, whether pivotal or cameo, becomes an integral part of his narratorial process. The plausibility of Johnny Gibbs' transition from a model student to a gang member is validated more with the haunting female image because it gives Johnny cause for some contemplation of conscience and/or moral retreat. In this context, the female is a positive agent. However, Arnold Rampersad's concluding analysis of female characters in the novella's afterword gives credence to Wright's continued marginality and negative treatment of them. For example, Johnny's decision to remain a runaway is confirmed when he finds out that his biological mother was a crazed, unwedded mother, who was forced to orphan him; he becomes convinced that he cannot trust the world of adults, especially women.

Though Rampersad catalogues the negative images of females in *Rite of Passage*, he also acknowledges Wright's inclination to characterize them positively. To Rampersad the haunting image of the woman at the end of the novella "presents a black woman standing for the finest qualities, those that make a difference between suffering and despair, on the one hand, and happiness and hope on the other. She is home" (127). And Johnny finally comes to the realization that "he yearned to sink to his knees to some kind old black woman and sob, "Help me . . . I can't go through with this!" (127).

By ending the story with the reverberating cry from the unidentified female who captured Johnny's attention with, "You Boys," Wright is using her as Johnny's conscience, and, thus, she is needed to provoke an even more sympathetic response to Johnny's situation when he responds "I can't go through with this;" even with her very sketchy characterization in the narrative, she reminds the reader that this young man has not forsaken his family values. As Rampersad asserts, she becomes "hope" and "home." But also she is simply a shadowy figure, a phantom, a final element that Wright uses to give closure to his narrative and, simultaneously, to confirm Johnny's moral conscience. The female character's role in the narrative demonstrates that Johnny has not sealed his membership in the gang; again, the female is needed for Wright's narratorial purpose––in this case—to leave Johnny with a more positive image. Wright's cycle in *Rite of Passage* is now complete, for he has begun the narrative with two females who are the stimulus for Johnny's entrance into gang culture and ended it with a female to suggest Johnny's exit from gang culture and return to home.

Gangs or buddies or male homosocialism, adolescent or adult, is an element in Wright's fiction that is significant in the context of race, gender, and sexuality. "Big Boy Leaves Home," *Native Son, The Outsider, The Long Dream,* and *Rite of Passage* are texts that present males interacting under myriad circumstances. Not only do Wright's tragic heroes live on the cutting edge (a few only barely escaping their death) but so do their buddies, some of whom meet tragic ends as in "Big Boy Leaves Home" and *The Outsider.* Regardless of the fate of Wright's males, most of them, while bonding, demonstrate enjoyment and humor, culminating in signifying or some type of banter, occasionally foreshadowing the conflict and or even death that awaits one or, as in "Big Boy Leaves Home," several of them.

The dynamics of male homosocialism in the beginning scene of *The Outsider* is similar to that in "Big Boy Leaves Home;" Cross Damon and his buddies have just completed a shift at the Post Office, and, like Big Boy and his buddies, Bobo, Lester, and Buck, enjoy the frolicking behavior, cajoling antics, signifying, etc. as they stand outside on a cold, snowy evening in Chicago. Though they are adult males, they are not shy of expressing their familiarity with each other with candor and physical contact (like Big Boy and his adolescent buddies). Wright's males naturally touch, and his description of their physical contact, the positioning of their bodies, as well as their dialogue, presents a male-to-male intimacy with homoerotic overtones that can also create a feminine effect.

Though females are the main cause of the initial conflict in *The Outsider* and become a cataclysmic agent for its dramatic conflict, it is the dynamics of the male's journey away from them, along with his mounting debt, that continue to develop the narrative. Females begin and intermittently comprise the narrative action, but Wright's main purpose in the text, as well as with most of his major male characters, is to present the plight of Cross Damon, the protagonist, who feigns his death after a subway train wreck. Using the identity of another African American male killed in the wreck, Cross puts his own identification on the body of a resembling dead black body and eventually boards a train to New York, assuming another identity as Lionel Lane. Wright presents Cross's journey thereafter as one who has experiences and relationships with both black and white and who "seeks to understand and analyze each experience and relationship in light of an entire social, political, and ideological system" (Graham xxiii), thus creating his fictional ideologue, *The Outsider*. In addition, Cross's homosocial experiences include his participation in a male group, which introduces the narrative, and a relationship he establishes with a white male after his escape. Although the use of the female is subdued as it develops, the situation of females forms the basis for Cross Damon's escape. Thus, Wright continues this technique of using the female as instigator for dramatic conflict and narrative action.

Femaleness is also conveyed in this type of homosocializing because Wright describes the dynamics of it with an interesting delicacy that takes its masculinity into a realm of intimacy often associated with heterosexual relationships. Wright's description of the male-to-male relations is similar to how a male responds to a female because of the intimacy that is transmitted with his specific phrasing and use of language. Moreover, it points to Eve Sedgwick's conceptualization of homosocial desire as cited earlier.

A close reading of Wright's articulation of male homosocialism in *The Outsider* will reveal how it is executed with such detail and delicacy. He introduces Cross and his friends with the statement, "On a South Side street four masculine figures moved slowly forward shoulder to shoulder and the sound of their feet trampling and sloshing in the melting snow echoed loudly" (1). The alliterative effect of the line gives the description a poetic quality and is followed by phrases and dialogue that present the physicality of their experience, especially as Wright's description continues, "They jostled each other with rude affection and their hot breaths projected gusts of vapor on to the chilled morning air" (1). The physical contact is initiated by Cross, who asks, "Booker, let me rest this tired old body on you, hunh" (1)? After Booker protests with a laugh, Cross then "turned and flung his arm about the shoulder of a big, fat, black man" named Joe, who not only refuses but also asks "Why pick on me" (1-2)? Cross responds, "Cause you're soft as a mattress and can stand it" (2). This physical contact and specific choice of words end when Cross "swiftly pulled the glove off his right hand and grabbing Pink's shoulder, rammed his bare fingers down the collar of Pink's neck" (2).

In this scene there is the juxtaposition of the feminine, i.e., "soft," arms being "flung around shoulders," and "fingers on a "neck," with the masculine, "Stand on your own two big flat feet," "Jesus! Your fingers' cold as *snakes*! . . . . They ought to call you *Mr. Death*" (2)! Moreover, the phrase "rude affection," has an oxymoronic effect, contrasting "harshness" with "softness" in a male homosocial context.

Historically, the criteria for male behavior in hetero/homophobic patriarchal societies require that physical contact between males occur in gender-specific situations, such as in traditionally-oriented male sports when it is absolutely necessary rather than in natural, carefree socializing. However, the homosocializing of Wright's male characters goes beyond the expectations of Western hetero/homophobic behavior with Cross and his buddies, who primarily exhibit rather intimate gesturing that, again suggests the homoerotic, as in the beginning scene of "Big Boy Leaves Home," the pool room scene with Bigger and Gus, and, most important, the masturbation scene with Bigger and Jack in the unexpurgated publication of *Native Son*.

It is this type of homosocializing that points to Sedgwick's conceptualization of homosocialism and male desire that represents the "entire continuum" of "the structures of men's relations with other men" (2). According to Sedgwick, the word "desire" is more appropriate in designating "the erotic emphasis . . . even when its manifestation is hostility or hatred or something less emotively charged, that shapes an important relationship" (2). Thus, Cross's relationships with various males he encounters are markedly different, some both racially and ideologically charged, but the male homosocialism with his buddies and the male-to-male relationship he establishes with Ely Houston, the New York District Attorney, demonstrate this concept of "male desire."

The Outsider continues with admonishments and chastisements that reveal the nurturing element also existing among Wright's males. Cross's friend Joe exclaims, "If you're cold, it's your own damn luck" . . . . "You don't take care of yourself . . . . "You drink too much. Don't eat enough . . . Don't sleep" (2). In contrast with the banter Cross and his buddies share in this beginning scene, this is a demonstration of caring, admonishing behavior, revealing the extent of their friendship beyond just work and play. It is this nurturing element that relates to Leslie Fieldler's comments regarding male escape in which he contends, "with the bulwark of woman left behind, the wanderer feels himself without protection, more motherless child than free man. To be sure, there is a substitute for wife or mother presumably waiting in the green heart of nature man, the good companion," (xxi) in other words, another male, as in Hawthorne's "Young Goodman Brown" and Irving's "Rip Van Winkle."

As Cross and his buddies walk toward their favorite tavern, The Salty Dog, he is reluctant to discuss his personal conflicts of a disgruntled, threatening wife, impregnated and harassing girlfriend, nagging mother, and mounting financial debt. Yet Joe, one of his buddies, takes the opportunity to resume the signifying, and since they have noticed Cross's increased drinking, Joe humorously announces to the group what he concocts as Cross's problems, "the four As: Alcohol. Abortions. Automobiles. And Alimony," (4), with two of the four dealing with females. In response, "Cross stood aloof as the others bent over giggling" (4). Also, as they reminisce, focusing on the jokes Cross has played on his friends and others in the past, Wright's description transmits this sense of intimacy their relationship suggests: "They laughed, looking at Cross with tenderness in their eyes" (7). This line, along with a series of phrases Wright uses to articulate this sense of intimacy his males have with each other, creates this homoerotic effect, for Wright has these males looking at each other with "tenderness in their eyes" (7). Regardless of the journey Cross will embark upon in the remaining pages of *The Outsider*, these verbal interchanges and the physicality of their bonding reveal the unique relationship they have with each other as males.

The phenomenon of a racialized male homosocial situation is demonstrated in *The Outsider* with the relationship between Cross and the New York District Attorney, Ely Houston, whom he meets on the train bound to New York. This particular meeting is another example of Fiedler's theory regarding male escape—this abandonment of the female and escape to the forest, only to embrace or enter into the companionship of another male or a fraternity of males, in this case the former in the character of Houston, who plays a major role in articulating Cross's descent into Wright's pit of existential hell. Cross has feigned his death because of the problems he acquired from his wife, impregnated girlfriend, and mother, as well as the burden of debt. Houston comprises Cross's major encounter with white males, followed by his relations and antagonisms with his white communist comrades, Blount and Hilton, whom he eventually murders. These two encounters are the most significant in the entire narrative, but the dialogue between Cross and Houston on the train to New York is a rather poignant one that, again, like the relationship Cross has had with his buddies at the beginning of the text, extends into a realm of closeness that has its uniqueness; it is more than simply two males, black and white, conversing with each other; there exists a special bond that he and Houston will engender, and it will resurface at the end of the novel.

First, the physicality of male-to-male bonding in this particular instance is engaged because of Houston's physical difference as a hunchback. Thus, Cross's handicap of blackness is leveled with Houston's handicap as a hunchback, whose superiority of whiteness is compromised because his physical difference, at this particular time, is considered a physical defect. Wright, then, lessens the edge Houston has on Cross and moves them closer into a more equalized bond, for Houston reveals to Cross that he, like "Negroes," knows what it is like to be an outsider because of this stigmatized physical difference, like Cross's blackness in a predominantly white society. Therefore, at their initial meeting, Cross "knew that Houston, in identifying himself with Negroes, had been referring to his deformity. Houston was declaring himself to be an outsider like Cross and Cross was interested, but kept his face passive to conceal it" (163).

Once Wright has established this equilibrium between the two men, who are joined by another white male, Father Seldon, the intellectualism of Wright's character, this well-read philosophy major and college dropout, must be exhibited. Of course, many of Cross's character traits reflect some of the specifics of Wright's own life, for he assigns Cross a job at the post office and then infuses in him the trait of a voracious reader, who is now given the chance to spill his brains. Moreover, Houston's perspective regarding the plight of "Negroes"--their becoming "centers of knowing"-- is juxtaposed with the pragmatism of Father Seldon, who retorts, "You are much too complicated, Ely . . . . All the colored people need is the right to jobs and living spaces" (165).

After Cross's articulation of the problem with Houston, the latter responds, "You're on the beam. Say, where did you go to school? Not that you learn things like that in school . . ." (165). Cross replies, "Fisk," recalling one of the oldest historic black colleges. Immediately, Cross begins to have feelings of paranoia, and thinking that Houston may be tracking him, "He rose, this was getting too close. He had to go and 'hug' his black secret" (165). Again, Wright's diction in this male setting has this effect of intimacy, for he uses the verb "hug" instead of "hide." This sense of snugness that surrounds Wright's male characters is homoerotic and conventionally associated with heterosexuality; instead, Wright presents it in a male homosocial setting.

Eventually, Cross leaves Houston to prevent what he thinks might be further scrutiny. But his leaving only piques Houston's interest since Cross has impressed him with his ideas and apparently made him feel comfortable; Houston states, "It's not often that one meets someone who can grasp ideas" . . . "you strike me as being a man of pretty cool judgment and having some insight into life" (169). However, prior to a series of comments Houston makes to convince Cross of his identification with the oppression of African American people, he makes a statement that reveals his own pejorative sense of blackness, which he equates with white deformity: "But they ought to be able to talk to me without fear . . . . After all, in a psychological sense, I'm a brother to them" (170).

Prior to this exchange, Wright's diction is consistent in expressing this delicacy associated with maleness. When Houston approaches Cross again to continue their dialogue after their initial meeting, he asks if he is disturbing Cross, who falsely exclaims, "Oh no!" (168). In the next sentence, Wright, referring to Cross, comments, "His body seemed suddenly to be made of soft, melting wax" (168). Wright's delicate imaging of Cross's masked identity as soft, melting wax implies fear, as well as femininity, and is oppositional to the normalcy of masculine description: hardness, toughness, confident trickery, etc. Therefore, behind this veil of male affableness with Houston is Cross's real fear, like that of Bigger, who feigns toughness and confidence with his buddies as they plan the Blum robbery when in reality he is afraid. Regarding his response to Houston's inquiry, Cross is characterized further as wanting "to laugh out loud. If the man only knew how lost and guilty and scared he was! How wrapped in anxiety . . ." (169)! Thus, Cross represents a cadre of Wright's males whose toughness is inconsequential because the reality of fear and desperation is gnawing at their existence: Dave Saunders in "Almos a Man" begs to own a pistol, only to be so frightened with it that he accidentally shoots Jenny the mule; Fred Daniels in "The Man Who Lived Underground" manages to outwit the police, but because of overriding fear, ended up being erroneously pursued and finally shot and killed by them, and Erskine Fowler, in *Savage Holiday*, experiences so much fear and anxiety with an accidental death, that he, like Bigger, is responsible for both an accidental death and premeditated murder.

At the end of *The Outsider*, after Cross has committed several murders to protect his feigned identity and after the woman he chooses to sincerely love, Eva Blount, commits suicide, Ely Houston reappears. The one male that Cross has impressed is now confronting him with the horror of his actions and his existence. Cross's reactions to his abandoned family Houston has been located to confirm his identity, and Houston's discovery of Eva Blount's suicidal death as a result of her awareness of Cross's murderous path cause disappointment and disgust because of the special, even sacred relationship he perceives as having with him. Interestingly, when the final confrontation between Houston and Cross occurs, Wright places the former in a rather reclining, close situation with Cross in the statement, "Houston looked around, found a chair, dragged it to the bed and eased his deformed body on to it, some two feet from Cross" (557). Also, to reiterate how special Houston coveted their friendship, he intimates to Cross the following:

> "After all Damon, as I told you on the train that morning,
> I'm close enough to you, being a hunchback, being an
> outsider, to know how some of your feelings and thought
> processes must go. In a sense, I'm your brother . . . . We
> men are not complete strangers on this earth. The world
> changes, but men are always the same. And especially
> the various basic types of men––and you are an ancient,
> fundamental type––run the same." (563)

Finally, one of the most poignant slices of dialogue between characters in Wright's fiction is the exchange between Houston and Cross at the end of the novel. After Houston surprises Cross by not arresting him on murders he can confirm Cross committing, Wright includes several statements that illustrate this close bond existing between the two males:

And Cross felt sweat running down his face;
It was on his chest, seeping down his arms.
Even his legs were wet. Suddenly he wanted
To beg this man not to leave him. (572)

Wright continues with the following: "Since Houston had laid his self-hate (speaking of Cross) and his self love so mockingly naked . . ." (574) and "Houston's voice seemed to be closer now and the tone had changed; it was the voice of a brother asking an urgent, confidential question" (584).

Regardless of Wright's voice of criticism of whites in his major fiction and even nonfiction, *The Outsider*, more than any text, presents a camaraderie between an African American male and white male that is perhaps unparalleled in twentieth century American fiction. Even the unnamed African American male protagonist in Ralph Ellison's *Invisible Man* and Jack, his communist brother, do not share the intensity of a relationship that Ely and Cross develop. Moreover, after Cross has been shot by his communist stalkers, who are avenging the murders they know he has committed, it is Houston who has the final conversation with him as he querulously attempts to uncover Cross's complex inner self and motivation for his actions. Houston's last question and Cross's last testament conclude the narrative and provide readers with the grotesque, horrific sophistication of Wright's artistry in presenting and ending this existential sojourn. Houston asks Cross, "But why? Try and tell me . . .," to which Cross responds, "Because in my heart . . . I'm . . . I'm innocent . . . . That's what made the horror . . ." (586).

NOTES

1   Sedgwick cites the definition of Heidi Hartmann in *Between Men* and proceeds to ask whether of not a relationship between Ronald Reagan and Jesse Helms, promoting the interests they share in public policy, is any way "congruent with the bond of a loving gay male couple" (3). Sedgwick continues by asserting that even gays would disgustedly say no. However, she proceeds to present another alternative approach to analyzing male-to-male relations, which she perceives as homosocial desire and homoeroticism.

2   The lines quoted from "Big Boy Leaves Home" are from The Library of America's 1991 publication, *Richard Wright, Early Works*, which includes *Lawd Today*, *Uncle Tom's Children* and *Native Son*. The short stories only are from *Uncle Tom's Children* in this publication. Quotes from *Native Son* and *Lawd Today* are from recent paperback editions.

3   In Jenkins' and Hine's anthology of essays on black masculinity, Robyn Wiegman has a definitive note on the mythology of the African American male as rapist and its implications in Wright's characterization of Bigger Thomas. Wiegman also comments on the victimization and lynching of African American males as a result of psychological and economic issues that define white masculinity and the protection of the white woman.

4   Claude Brown's 1965 publication, *Manchild in the Promise Land*, is often thought of as a replication of Wright's *Black Boy*. Brown's autobiography depicts his days as a juvenile delinquent who was eventually sent to a children's correctional institution, the Wiltwyck School for Boys, in upstate New York. Wright had an interest in this same institution while gathering material for *Native Son*. Prior to his residency in New York, he had worked with the Southside Boys Club in Chicago. Wright's daughter, Julia Wright, commented (during a conference in Paris, France on Black Expatriates) that her father was interested in juveniles and gang culture. *Rite of Passage*, posthumously published in 1994, is a text that specifically reflects this interest.

CHAPTER 3

Richard Wright's Treatment Of The White Female Character

Scenarios involving the element of surprise and awkwardness accompany Richard Wright's treatment of the white female character. This type of discord often creates racial conflict and ambivalence, feelings of both hate and desire. In essence, the white female character, more than her African American female counterpart, often creates and, especially, exacerbates the tragic consequences of Wright's males, especially the African American ones. The white female character, more often than not, is one who immediately creates the conflict and the drama involving the male character. Thus, one observes an obvious pattern, a definite formula, Wright creates with this character, who is also pivotal to the narrative's structure.

Mary Dalton's centrality in *Native Son* has, according to Alan France, "become an absence, a silence that Irigaray believes patriarchal discourse always means when it inscribes woman: women are trapped in a system of meaning which serves the auto-affection of the (masculine) subject (qtd. in France 421). In the case of Richard Wright, it is a discourse of masculinity that evolves from the African American male's sojourn in a historically white racist patriarchal society. Thus, an angry or disenfranchised African American male becomes the nexus of Wright's texts, and most analyses address those themes emanating from the dynamics of his male experiences. However, femaleness sets off maleness in the narrative, and the white female character is the stimulus for Wright's sequencing of events that formulate the plots and subplots in his narratives. One observes Bigger's immediate annoyances with Mary and perceives her accidental death as having a dichotomous effect: it sets off an unfortunate set of circumstances that produce an inevitable result, and it anticipates Bigger's fate, the fate of an African American male connected to a white woman in 1940s America. Often it is a fate that is difficult for African American males to escape regardless of their socioeconomic prominence. Abdul JanMohamed contends "Wright brilliantly investigates the economy of castration in his last novel, *The Long Dream*, but in *Native Son*, where he is just beginning to explore the problematic of racialized sexuality, he casts it in terms of rape" (107-08). JanMohamed continues, "While the novel intends to depict how Bigger can surmount the debilitating effects of racism, it demonstrates in fact that the phallocratic order can foreclose effective forms of resistance and can position some black males in such a way that they are incapable of asserting their 'manhood' against racism except by replicating phallocratic violence against women" (108). More specifically, Mary and Bigger become victims of an external set of circumstances, but Bigger must pay the price regardless of his innocence regarding the charge of rape, i.e., penetration. According to JanMohamed, regardless of gender, "the racialized subject is always already constructed as a 'raped' subject in Wright's view" (109). In other words, even Bigger, the accused rapist, is both socially and psychologically raped by the larger society.

Even though Mary remains the ultimate cause of Bigger's subsequent fate, the only "legalized" definition of rape occurs with Bessie, as suggested by JanMohamed who contends that "Bigger's gruesome rape and murder of his black companion. Bessie is utilized by both the narrative and white society as a substitute for the supposed rape of Mary. The court argues that if he raped Bessie, he must have raped Mary too and succeeds in convicting him though it lacks evidence that he committed the act" (110). Moreover, Mary Dalton is Wright's quintessential female character. This analysis proposes that the interactions between Bigger and Mary create a paradigm that most white female and African American relations in Wright's novels fit. This paradigm is created by Wright's narrative technique, which includes the situation or scenario of the accidental—the surprise—an awkwardness accompanying the entrance of the white female character in the narrative. Following Wright's world of incongruence and discord—black/white relations in American society—is the tragic fatalism of the African American male and, in most instances, unsurprisingly, the tragic end of his white female characters. This attests to Wright's continuous use of tumultuous forces that lead to destruction—his gothic approach.

This element of surprise and awkwardness is very clearly demonstrated in Wright's earliest short story, "Big Boy Leaves Home." After Wright presents his pastoral setting with Big Boy and his friends, Lester, Bobo, and Buck, enjoying the peaceful, warm countryside environment, they surprisingly encounter a white female, who, as stated earlier, turns their world around and creates their tragic fate—death and flight from an angry white mob. Wright's use of mischievous juveniles, which also implies gang culture, is juxtaposed with the innocence and naiveté of young boys (the idyllic moment) who experience oneness with nature and the feeling that "all is right with the world." However, again, Wright presents a tabooed situation by having the white woman unexpectedly amble upon nude young black boys warming their bodies after a swim in a creek owned by a white man, "Ol Man Harvey." As trespassers, they are stunned, mortified by the sight of a person who represents their most horrid fears—a white female. How should they act? What should they do?

Just as Bigger is shocked, stunned in his enclosed space—Mary's bedroom in which the Blind Mrs. Dalton surprisingly enters—Big Boy and his buddies find themselves entrapped in the outdoors. Ironically, it is not the physical entrapment that presents their greatest risk; it is the presence of whiteness, more specifically white femaleness that constitutes entrapment—a continuum in Wright's fiction most dramatically imaged in the rat scene at the beginning of *Native Son*. One realizes that because of the African American male's intolerable presence in the patriarchal terrain, most situations outside of his own community hold the potential for entrapment. It is this type of entrapment that Wright uses with several of his protagonists, e.g., Mann in "Down by the Riverside," Fishbelly in *The Long Dream*, and Carl Owens in "The Man of All Work" in *Eight*

Men. Even Fred Daniels in "The Man Who Went Underground" is in flight initially because he is being accused of raping a white woman. Ironically, Daniels' entrapment consists of a living in an underground sewer hole that affords him a surreal freedom he uses to mock the real world above ground. Though he avoids capture and escapes into a sewer hole, he is finally caught and killed at the end of the narrative.

Nevertheless, just as Wright gives Bigger a few seconds to contemplate an escape, i.e., to get by the blind Mrs. Dalton without her detecting him in Mary's bedroom, he endows Big Boy with this same forethought—an attempt by the naked boys to circumvent the white female, get their clothes, and flee. The reader is intensely drawn into this moment of suspense, realizing that if this doesn't happen, tragedy follows. Big Boy is just as awkward as Bigger, and as overwhelmed with fear. He makes his plea . . . "Lady, we wanna git our cloes . . . his words coming mechanically" (250). However, like Bigger, he experiences fear and indecisiveness. Though Bobo "ran and snatched the clothes" (250), his actions are too late, and all are caught by the white female's fiancée, Ol Man Harvey's son, who, hearing screams, rushes to her defense with a rifle that Big Boy eventually takes possession of to prevent the entire group from being killed; the white man has already killed two, Lester and Bobo.

At this point in the narrative, one can observe that Big Boy's verbal desperation is akin to Bigger's nonverbal but physical repetitive thrusts with the pillow that eventually smothers Mary to death. Again, Wright meticulously and mechanistically uses language and actions with characters to create serious dramatic effect. Thus, Wright's narrative technique with the female character is carefully drawn and strategically defined to underscore what Mohamed terms as the African American male's social death and what Michael Best terms as lynch law, which he contends is "deterministic because the final outcome is, under all conditions of the law, the only possible outcome—'summary justice' for threatening white masculinity, and the charge of upholding the purity of southern white womanhood" (118 Best).

There are certainly multiple explanations and theories regarding the vehement anger and belligerence provoked in white males when an

African American male is socially/sexually connected to a white female. Historically, European and European American slaveholders, instilled with the process of commercialism and commodities exchange, viewed black male bodies as a prized possession to effect capital gains. Parallel to this ownership of blacks was the same ownership and control of the white female, who according to social criteria, was deemed as the white male's most prized possession, yielding the most valued offspring like himself, white males who will continue white male patriarchal traditions. For the African American male to either involuntarily or voluntarily insert himself into this equation, outside of his designated terrain, is to upset the logic of the white male enterprise. Thus, the wrath of the sole possessor of the black male and white female must be aimed at the brazen black aggressor—whose only position during enslavement was to provide free labor for whites.

In "Big Boy Leaves Home" the white female escapes injury and death; instead, the white male is killed. However, the white male's reaction and subsequent actions result in the loss of three black lives. Big Boy survives but not without a very risky, life threatening escape. In fact, the white vengeance that is unsuccessful with Big Boy is successful with his family, who are victimized by the burning and ultimate destruction of their home. While Big Boy is in hiding, he hears voices regarding the fate of his family, "We looked all thu the shack n couldn't fin hide ner hair of im. Then we drove the ol woman and man out n set the shack on fire . . . . Yuh shoulda heard the ol nigger woman howl . . ." (268).

In most of the tragedy that occurs regarding African American life, Wright's technique of spontaneity, of surprise, defines the white woman as instigator, the primary agent that creates all the carnage and destruction unfolding and culminating in the narrative. Wright creates an awkward, discomforting, and eventually tragic moment for four African American boys, yet at the core of the entire narrative's dramatic conflict as instigator is the white female; she sets off the action and deepens it. Also, in this particular case, just as in Mary's, the white female's initial actions are not malevolently caused, but in 1930s America, the sight of four naked African American boys causes her to have an involuntary reaction.

Juxtaposing African American males and white females continues in Wright fiction even after he leaves the south and writes his last novel in France, The *Long Dream*, which is another major work that presents an unsavory characterization of the white female. Published in 1958 toward the end of Wright's life, readers encounter an African American male protagonist, in this case Fishbelly (Fish), whose responses to white women are ambivalent. Set in the South and presenting an eclectic agenda on black/white relations, this novel fits a similar pattern with Wright's females; within the first fifty pages of the text, the white female initiates the action. Mrs. Tucker, Fishbelly's mother, informs him of the tragic consequence of one of his friends and idols, Chris when she states, "It was Chris son" his mother whimpered. "They caught im in the hotel with a white girl" (61). Chris's violent end as a result of his relationship with a white woman parallels Wright's own account of African American males losing their lives because of their illicit connections with whites or simply going beyond the racial boundaries. A young Wright states, "A dread of white people now came to live permanently in my feelings and imagination . . ." (*Black Boy* 85). He further adds, "I had never been abused by whites, but I had already become as conditioned to their existence as though I had been the victim of a thousand lynchings" (87).

Fishbelly and his friends experience extreme fear when they encounter a white woman at the fair who bears her breast to them as she solicits. She hollers, "Come closer, Don't be afraid, I'll take you in for five dollars a piece," while "unbuttoning her blouse and baring her big white breast in the half light" (44). This offer, of course, frightens Fishbelly and his friends, Zeke and Tony. It takes them by surprise and immediately creates a shocking, awkward situation; they realize that being in the presence of such a spectacle has the potential for danger. While this particular case proves harmless (they quickly move on at the fair), it is an example of a sudden and threatening surprise instigated by a white female.

Even though Fishbelly and his buddies are aware of the white female's dangerous, deadly sting, they cannot avoid playing with their fate as young boys who will quickly, without forethought, throw caution to the wind. Another episode includes Fishbelly and his buddies playing around in the basement of his family's funeral home during his father's absence. Because the location of the basement's window is parallel to the sidewalk, they mischievously decide to scare women who pass by them, one being a white female. After scaring her from a window and watching her go into what seems to be a convulsive fall on the sidewalk, they immediately realize the possible danger of their actions for a good laugh. Finally, with the grip of fear and terror, they make the following resolution:

> "Jeeeeesus," Zeke whispered. "Let's don't scare
> no more folks," Sam said. "Come on . . . ."
> He shut the window. They groped in the dark,
> filled with a sense of another world stretching
> out there in the silent night —a white world. (50)

In "Sexual Initiation and Survival in Richard Wright's *The Long Dream*," Earl V. Bryant writes "most of the text's criticism tends to focus on Fish's sexual initiation," and critics have not devoted enough sufficient attention to Fishbelly's sexual initiation as "an absolute prerequisite for his survival in the white world" (57). Bryant's analysis basically reveals how, through the process of sexual initiation, orchestrated by Fish's father, Tyree, Wright creates a situation in which what is most forbidden is most desired: the white female. Moreover, often cited in Wright scholarship is Bigger's feeling of exaltation after killing Mary, the sacred possession of the white male that he has clandestinely destroyed. However, Fishbelly has been judicially and discursively warned about the constant threat of death that an African American man faces in relation to a white woman. After Chris has been killed by white vigilantes, Tyree vehemently warns Fishbelly. He states, ". . . Fish, the main thing for a black man is to live and not end up like Chris. Most folks on this earth don't even have to think about dying like that. But we do. For most folks to die like that's a accident. For us, that accident comes too damned often to be called a accident" (73).

Regardless of the father's admonitions, Wright imbues in Fishbelly's character this ambivalent fascination with white females, for after he hears of Chris's death, this protagonist seems to have a fixation with them that he finds difficult to shed. He snatches a picture of a sparsely clad white woman from an old stack of newspapers in the bathroom of his father's funeral business and jams it into a pocket. He thinks, "He didn't know why he had done that; he had acted before he had been aware of it. But he knew that he wanted to look at that face again and he would never be able to stop thinking of what had happened to poor Chris until he had solved the mystery of why that laughing white face was so radiantly happy and at the same time charged with dark horror" (64). Chris's death instills in Fishbelly a curiosity that haunts him throughout his development as a young man. Thus, Wright's *The Long Dream*, which could certainly be labeled as a coming of age novel, a bildungsroman, is as much about the African American male's fascination with the white female and whiteness (both son and father have light-skinned African American girlfriends) as it is his victimization by the white power structure. There is no doubt that Fishbelly realizes the danger of being associated with a white female, yet he seems to involuntarily or perhaps even voluntarily initiate actions that suggest otherwise—his desire for her.

Fishbelly's ambivalence toward the white female relates to a similar situation cited in another Wright text, the short story, "The Man Who Killed a Shadow," in *Eight Men*. In an essay on this particular story, Neal A. Lester argues America's relative passivity toward female victimization via language in the music industry.[1] In this context, Lester alludes to Franz Fanon's analysis of race and sexuality and the fantasy of some white women, "A Negro is raping me" (qtd. in Lester 6). Lester contends that there is this prevailing view that "confuses the aggression of mutual consensual sexual intimacy with aggressive sexual assault" (6). After presenting a litany of what is viewed as obscene and violent lyrics from popular culture, especially the music community of gangster rap, Lester asserts . . . "this same attitude prevails among those who see Wright's story as another instance of a white woman consciously manipulating a black man because of the racial gender-specific sexual myths that have created them both" (6). Lester disagrees with this popularized view, and his analysis of a virginal white librarian killed by a black janitor (Saul) is grounded in the following supposition:

> . . . Wright's story is less about Saul's victimization
> by a white female than by his warped initiation into
> manhood through sexual violence, violent sex, and

> sexual fantasy. Saul's psychological confusion about
> the violent act he commits reiterates his dangerous
> social perpetuation of the myth of the black
> male rapist, a myth that prescribes real or
> imagined intimacy with a white woman--
> in its myriad forms and possibilities--as a
> definitive performance of black masculinity. (6)

Though Fishbelly's sojourn in *The Long Dream* fits Wright's fictional formula of African American male challenges and battles with the white power structure, this male's saga with the white female becomes as France states, "the alterity of the text," because readers initially are lured into the narrative action with a situation involving this particular character and because of Fishbelly's ambivalence toward her. Also, even though *The Long Dream's* major plot deals with Tyree Tucker's illegal connections with corrupt and racist policemen, crucial to the novel are several episodes of Fishbelly with white females, who cunningly pose life threatening risks. However, Fishbelly becomes aware of this threat and its potential for tragic consequences, and Wright characterizes him with this disposition of uncertainty, of ambivalence toward them.

Other threatening scenarios involving white females and Fishbelly's dubious behavior toward them begin when he and his buddies are mimicking war in the woods—land that belongs to whites, which, of course, presents a violation of trespassing. This is a similar setting to that of "Big Boy Leaves Homes." Wright narrates, "Eight black bodies flashed in the sun against the yellow-brown mud . . . . Eight pair of hands began a frantic scooping up of mud, which was rounded into balls and stacked behind trees selected as fortresses" (98). After Fishbelly and his comrades have their attacks and victoriously flee from the opponents, he and one friend, Tony, are caught on the land by two local policemen, "Fishbelly spun about and saw two white policemen bearing down upon him with drawn guns" (100). On the boys' way to being arrested, the two police officers stop to have a soda. While the officers are being served by a white waitress, Fishbelly finds himself staring at her with remembrances of his friend

Chris, "Fishbelly stared at the girl's white face, her pink cheeks, her [rubby-red] lips, and her sky-blue eyes—and he remembered Chris . . . . The world he saw was *alluring* but *menacing*" (101). Fishbelly is, therefore, haunted by the social taboo, lynch law, and the reality of a social death. Wright creates a quagmire of events that place Fishbelly's life constantly on the cutting edge in interracial interactions, most of which involve white females and dangerously intimidating white males. After one of the police officers catches Fishbelly staring at the white waitress, he makes vehement threats. They end with him facetiously stating, "Nigger, I'm going to castrate you!" (102).

Having been taunted by the white policemen, who frighten him so much that he faints, Fishbelly and his friends are taken in for questioning, only for the purpose of being ridiculed. Fishbelly is viewed as soft by them (to them an oddity in comparison to most African American males) because he is so quickly prone to fainting. While enroute to jail, he realizes in his possession is the picture of a white woman. Frightened at the thought of being caught with it, he thinks, "creased and tucked into his tattered billfold was the frayed photograph of that laughing white woman wearing only panties and a brassiere—that photograph that he had impulsively torn out of the newspaper in the toilet on the night that Chris had been killed" (104). In terror, he is able to swallow the picture before he and his friend are taken to jail for continued harassment instead of legal charges. In this novel, Wright is continuously flirting with the black male/white female syndrome he creates in his fiction.

Tyree Tucker's illicit relations with corrupt cops cause two major tragedies in the novel: a nightclub fire that takes a large number of African American lives because of ignored fire code violations and his own murder for not producing the evidence of payoffs, the cancelled checks he paid the corrupt police officer, Cantley. One of the final episodes in *The Long Dream* occurs when Fishbelly refuses to tell Cantley where the checks are that his father kept for evidence of payoffs. After Cantley realizes that his threatening tactics aimed at Fishbelly (after Tyree's death) fail, he uses what is often viewed as the white male's most strategic weapon against African American males, the white female. Fishbelly has clandestinely secured the checks from his father's mulatto girl friend, Gloria, and is awaiting the perfect time to incriminate Cantley in order to escape. However, a white woman, claiming she was sent by one of Fishbelly's African American female friends, comes to his apartment. Detecting that this is some type of entrapment, Fishbelly leaves her in his apartment while he goes to summon the police chief, Cantley, who coincidentally is in the area. While Fishbelly is explaining to Cantley how this mysterious white woman has forced her way into his apartment, other officers approach the woman and then inform Cantley that she has accused Fishbelly of raping her. Fishbelly is imprisoned, and after realizing his entrapment, he "sank to the floor and stared listlessly. He had never seen the girl before, yet he had lived with an image and a sense of her almost all the days he had been alive. *Oh Gawd, why hadn't he fled*" (320)? This scene, along with others in the *Long Dream*, causes the novel often to be labeled as one of Wright's weakest, with most responses suggesting Wright's loss of artistic effectiveness as a result of his long expatriation in France and unawareness of a changing south.

Fishbelly does flee after a very intense imprisonment where he is fighting what is finally conceded as a trumped up rape charge. He is able to submit the cancelled checks as evidence of police bribes to a less threatening District Attorney, who is determined to expose corruption among the police and prosecute the violators. Finally, Fishbelly, unlike most of Wright's protagonists, prevails and escapes injury and death, after having very close, as well as life threatening encounters with white females.

As in *The Long* Dream, the white female as instigator continues in *Savage Holiday*, one of Wright's later and most ignored novels. Margaret Walker Alexander includes it in her repertoire of Wright's texts to further explain his complexity as a writer. She is emphatic in labeling *Savage Holiday* as one of his most sadistic and misogynistic texts and claims that the most extreme violence against a female character occurs in the novel. She contends, "He regards the woman Mabel Blake, mother of the dead boy, Tony, as degraded, and like all the women in his fiction she is whore, cunt, bitch—the fallen woman" (Walker 247). Walker Alexander further comments that this text is a reflection of Wright's own torn psyche, his tormented childhood fears haunting him.

In *Savage Holiday*, Wright presents the unfortunate circumstances of his protagonist, Erskine Fowler, a white male (in fact, all of the characters in *Savage Holiday* are white) who experiences a forced retirement form his top level position in an insurance corporation and finds himself faced with the unexpected fate of "enforced leisure" (34). Next door to Fowler's Manhattan tenth story apartment is the war-widowed mother, Mabel Blake, and her five—year old son, Tony. It is this circumstance of the young boy that will create a major dramatic conflict in *Savage Holiday*. Again, readers encounter an awkward, accidental surprise occurrence. Little Tony Blake accidentally falls from his tenth floor balcony after being shockingly led to the edge of a faulty ledge because of a surprise sighting of a naked Fowler. The naked sighting occurs because Fowler accidentally is locked outside of his apartment after taking a shower, opening his apartment door, and awkwardly trying to reach for the Sunday paper. The locked door slams shut, and the subsequent episode has a quasi comic effect as the nude Fowler tries to determine how to get back into his apartment unseen. The reader can anticipate something happening, and according to the Wrightsian formula, it will not be positive. As Walker Alexander states earlier in *Daemonic Genius*, Wright is just as much influenced by Gothicism as he is by naturalism and existentialism.

However, even before the accidental death of little Tony Blake, Wright's love/hate formula begins to unfold with Fowler's matricidal comments concerning his mother and Mabel Blake. He equates Mabel's frequent male company with that of his mother during his own childhood and views both women as neglecting their sons. Very early in the novel when Fowler learns that sometimes little Tony is left alone at night, he thinks, "Women who couldn't give the right kind of attention to children oughtn't to be allowed to have them . . ." (35). One critic states, "Fowler, the reader learns, has had little contact with women during his life; he is both haunted by the memory of a mother who was much like Mabel and trapped by the compulsive conventionality of his stodgy sanctimonious Christianity. Her fate is sealed when, near the novel's end, in answer to Fowler's question as to how she could not love her son, she says, 'it's not in my nature to be a mother' and

'Erskine, I'm no mother.' What a cold monster of a woman! Erskine thinks before he murders her" (Early 229).

Also, as Fowler's hatred toward Mabel develops, the awkward, surprising event that causes little Tony's death is the immediate stimulus for Fowler's psychological trauma and eventual destruction of Mabel and himself. An interesting phenomenon with much of Wright's fiction is that it is the accidental, the incidental, what could be considered minutiae, that creates the larger than life dramatic effect in his narratives: Bigger and the pillow with Mary; the accidental encounter with Big Boy and his friends; the accidental shooting of the mule by Dave Saunders in "Almos a Man;" and the accidental train wreck in *The Outsider*. Little Tony Blake's accidental death, caused by his surprised sighting of Fowler, provides the drama for the disposition Fowler acquires toward Mabel, for he eventually begins to view her as a promiscuous and unfit mother.

Moreover, just as the white female is presented as an ominous agent in *Native Son*, "Big Boy leaves Home," and *The Long Dream*, Wright's characterization of Mabel via Fowler's thoughts, reduces the possibility of a sympathetic characterization of her. She enters the narrative after Wright has presented the severed ego of Erskine Fowler, following his forced retirement. Thus, even the male white Fowler achieves sympathetic parity with Wright's other African American males, for he intricately designs their violation. Fowler, no longer preoccupied with the challenges of work, becomes more sensitized to his surroundings, especially his neighbor Mabel and her son. In fact, Mabel becomes the scapegoat of Fowler's angry reaction toward the loss of his job and his mother. Mabel is, according to Decosta Willis's interpretation of Wright's female characters, the fallen angel, like most of the women Wright encounters in his boyhood and manhood, as well as those he creates in his fiction. Before little Tony's accident, Fowler thinks:

> She's sleeping and she lets that child bang and yell at this
> hour of the morning . . . . The child's voice ceased and he
> tucked his head into his pillow and drifted into a semi-
> dream state, thinking of Tony who, in turn, made him

> recall dimly his own, faraway childhood. Yes, he too has
> once romped and played alone, ... (38)

However, in addition to Fowler's feelings of disgust with Mary, the reader recognizes an equally compelling emotion of intrigue and infatuation. Fowler's thoughts of disdain are juxtaposed with such thoughts as, . . . "Mrs. Blake—alone, sensual, impulsive—was so much as he remembered his own mother that he found himself scolding her and brooding over her in his mind" (38). The Oedipal complex is so clearly embedded in this tale. It is further commented that "through a combination of guilt, fear, and sexual attraction, Fowler becomes involved with Mabel, one of Wright's intriguing female creations" (Early 229). One could add that Fowler's intrigue with Mabel is second to that of Cross Damon's with Eva Blount, the white female character, in *The Outsider.*

Regardless of how much emphasis Wright places on the plight of African American males in the context of victimization, especially caused by the white female, this intrigue develops into fear, followed by anger, and culminates in unbridled hate. One reviewer of *Savage Holiday* states, "Shying away from the racial problem he depicted in his other works, he writes here a riveting study in psychological fiction" (book jacket). And just as Wright creates the existential novel, *The Outsider,* he experiments with Freudian psychology in *Savage Holiday,* as well as in *The Long Dream.* Erskine Fowler's love/hate stance with his mother and then Mabel in *Savage Holiday* becomes intermittently woven into a mystery caused by Tony Blake's accidental death. Even though the first death is accidental, the intentional second death, Mabel's murder, is most vehemently executed, for it is treated just as heinously as Mary's decapitation and cremation in *Native Son.*

Even if the white female character does or does not survive, Wright's formula of blameful instigator applies. Besides Mabel's neglect of her son as her character flaw, her son's ten-story fall to his death becomes a symbolic indicator of Mabel as the fallen woman. She contributes to the fall and demise of her male counterpart, just as the cameo, sudden appearance of the white female does in "Big Boy," the situation of Mary in *Native Son* and the white females in *The Long Dream*, as well as that of the suicidal Eva Blount in *The Outsider*. Wright creates a situation with Tony's accident to further emphasize the negative, fatalistic presence of the white female, who regardless of her intention, in most instances invites nothing but trouble.

The Outsider certainly repeats this causal function of the white female character; however, there is an altering that occurs in this narrative because the protagonist becomes friends with the white female character, yet despite the warmth of their relationship, she does not survive. Once Cross Damon, *The Outsider's* protagonist, survives a train wreck, feigns his identity, murders a colleague, manages to rid himself of a white prostitute, and joins the communist party, he meets the captivating Eva Blount. She enters Cross Damon's life just as several white females do in Wright's own disclosed extramarital affairs. Wright's canon suggests that traditionally there are probably two types of white females that African American males encounter: the ones that are the primary cause for the troubles, incarceration, and lynching of African American men, "the white bitch," and the ones that set off a mutual attraction––the ones that African American men are sexually intimate with, perhaps fall in love with, and marry. Eva Blount represents the latter; she reigns as Wright's most complex female character, even more than Mary Dalton and Mabel Black. Mary Dalton becomes to Bigger the superficial white liberal who, as stated earlier, is more annoying than ingratiating. And Mabel Black is a stereotype, defined more by the thoughts and opinions of Erskine Fowler than her own dialogue and actions in the narrative; she prevails primarily as the unfit mother, who is directly the cause of her son's death. Even though Wright uses all white characters in *Savage Holiday*, his strategy of use, repudiation, and discard occurs with Mabel as with other white female characters in his racialized fiction.

Eva Blount, however, deviates from Wright's typical white female imaging in most of his works. Here again one observes Wright's use of the awkward entré with Eva Blount. Cross Damon's discomfort is apparent, and Wright is able to present the infatuation, the chemistry, that exists between the two. But the reader will eventually witness the demise of the white Eva Blount as the demise of the African American female characters.

Regardless, Wright's tersely favorable description of Eva suggests that she is special, particularly to Cross who, before leaving Chicago for New York, encounters a white prostitute who is abandoned. Realizing the challenges he already faces with his fake death and feigned identity, he, through deception, finds a way to escape her and proceed with his plan to go to New York; Cross realizes out of all the baggage (fraud, debt, and even murder) he has acquired for his escape, a white female will do nothing but invite trouble and jeopardize his plans.

However, when Cross, who is now Lionel Lane, shakes Eva's hands, he thinks, "an incredibly soft, white hand" (238). Afterwards, Wright presents the following descriptive passage as a suggestion of their attraction to each other.

> . . . his nostrils were full of the delicate perfume that she wore. He stared straight ahead of him, feeling that his life had at last touched something that stirred him to his depths. (238)

Syntactically, the reader can assume that this last phrase suggests that the "something" is Eva Blount, but Cross has been intensely scrutinized and interrogated by her husband, Gil. Therefore, this statement could also be referring to the total communist experience of meeting both Eva and Gil Blount. Nonetheless, Eva exudes a positive uniqueness in Wright's characterization of her, creating quite a contrast to his treatment of other white female characters.

Another indicator of the special place Eva will hold in the remaining days of Cross's life is his antagonism with Gil. Cross ". . . wondered how on earth had she come to be married to a coarse, inhuman character like Blount. Cross now shifted his gaze to Gil and was chagrined to find that Gil had been observing his observation of Eva" (238). When the two of them are alone, Cross has the opportunity to experience a certain intimacy with her, and eventually finds that she is a frustrated woman, married to a man who she feels has betrayed her in the interest of the Party. In fact, he is able to detect a certain nervousness on her part even when they first meet. He observes, "When his gaze met her, she smiled and looked off. She seemed tense, yet rigidly contained. She was a fragile girl of about twenty-four" (238).

Wright intensifies the relationship between Cross and Eva when Cross moves in with the Blounts, thus, creating a situation for him to pry clandestinely into Eva's diary, which reveals to him her inner strife as an artist and, more specifically, her recognition of being manipulated by the Party and her husband, Gil. After reading through Eva's notes while she and her husband are absent from the apartment, Cross reads Eva's last entry on him: "Colored people are so trusting and naïve . . . . He's going to be misled by Gil, just as I have been . . . (285). Cross realizes:

> Here was a lost, brave woman who has enough sensitivity
> to understand what he had to say. She was a victim like
> he; the difference was a willing victim and she was an
> involuntary one . . . . She protested and he said yes. And a
> world yawned between his yes and her no . . . . (285)

Thinking further of Eva, Cross wants to help her. In fact, he kills for her. After a threatening confrontation with the Blount's landlord, Herndon, Cross is provoked not only into killing this man who has become an enemy but also Eva's husband Gil. Both men are killed simultaneously without Eva's knowledge. And the aftermath of these two killings, along with others in the novel, causes Wright's protagonist, like Dostoyevsky's Roskolnikov, to have a deep sense of despair and a compelling urge to confess his murders to a person he trusts and feels rather close to, in Cross's case, Eva Blount. After she becomes aware of the murders, especially that of her husband, Gil, Cross finds himself "holding Eva's hand, desiring her body. And the wall of deception which he had begun to erect to conceal the nature of her husband's death would throw her, perhaps, into his arms . . ." (318).

Moreover, one of the final scenes Cross has with Eva reveals the compassion—the love—that each feels for the other. After he thinks that he has escaped suspicion of murder, Eva intimates to Cross, "if you leave, I shall kill myself" (382). Toward the end of the novel, they vow their love for each other, for Eva says to Cross in a whisper, "Tell me darling . . . is it wrong to love so soon like this?" (435). But there is no consummation of their love; they are never sexually linked. However, as events unfold, and Eva is made aware of Cross's vehement deception (not being Lionel Lane and, instead, a serial murderer), she commits suicide by leaping from a window. Finally, it is Cross's afterthoughts that further define the love he has for this woman, . . . "already he was feeling what he had been grasping for in his loving her. That capacity for him to suffer had seized upon this lovely, frail girl as the representation and appearance in life of what he felt had to be protected and defended" (542). Eva's death, therefore, is the defining moment of Cross's self realization; she represented the last vestige of true human emotion Cross was able to cultivate after having to mask so much of himself. After experiencing his journey of lies, deception, and desperation, and especially loss of Eva, Wright's protagonist is left to create another reality of the self—an existential self of aloneness.

Wright's altered and more positive treatment of another African American male and white female relationship recurs in two other short stories, "Bright and Morning Star" in *Uncle Tom's Children* and "Big Black Good Man" in *Eight Men*. Wright's propagandistic strategies are enacted, and he presents his ultimate vision of racial harmony with a rather familial portrayal of the African American mother, her son, and the white female. In addition, instead of the white female putting an African American male's life at risk, she risks her own life in order to inform Johnny-Boy, her boy friend, and Aunt Sue, his mother, of a leak concerning a clandestine communist meeting. A white informant and feigned communist, Booker, is a spy for local white authorities. When Reva expresses her fear regarding Johnny-Boy's delay in reaching home, Aunt Sue thinks, "Yeah; its something about the party er Johnny-Boy thas gone wrong. . . . Lawd, Ah wondah ef her pa knows how she feels bout Johnny Boy?" Reva and Aunt Sue become mother and daughter—Wright's rebellious, revolutionary portrayal of the South despite the politics of the time. Aunt Sue continues to think of Reva as special, and the latter's relationship with Johnny-Boy represents a new day, for Aunt Sue ". . . liked Reva; the brightest glow her heart had ever known was when she had learned that Reva loved Johnny-Boy. But beyond Reva were cold white faces. Ef theys caught it means *death* . . ." (414).

However, Wright returns to this pattern of ridding his narrative of significant characters, with the deaths of Johnny-Boy and Aunt Sue. Interestingly, the author presents a life threatening relationship in the old South, that of the African American male and white female, yet it is Johnny-Boy and the elderly black woman who become the sacrificial lambs. It is this tragic consequence that points to the masochistic Wright, which perhaps a critic like Walker Alexander validly views as his self hate, created by racism, poverty, and violence, as well as a dysfunctional familial environment.

Reva's imaging in "Bright and Morning Star" recalls another nonthreatening white female character who establishes a consensual relationship with an African American male character and, unWrightsian-like, they live happily ever after. Wright's "Big Black Good Man" is a story in which, aside from the positive dynamic that exists in the relationship between the big black good man and a white prostitute by the name of Lena, there is an altered presentation of racism. Olaf, a puny white American hotel manager and naval retiree residing in Copenhagen, is intimidated and eventually terrified by a different type of black male.

Wright presents to his readers a larger than life, extremely black male, who is well dressed, assertive, and possesses plenty of money. Olaf, who exhibits a paternalistic attitude toward young sailors and black patrons, is fearfully disconcerted by the "big black man's" direct questions: "I want a bottle of whiskey and a woman ...", "Can you fix me up?" and "You send the whiskey and the woman quick, pal" (99)? However, Olaf's characterization of the "big black man" is in direct contrast to the comments Lena, a prostitute makes. His prejudice is juxtaposed with Lena's nonracialized and unbiased responses, for when Olaf warns Lena by stating, "But this one is big," she retorts, "He's just a man," and "She didn't give a good goddamn about how big and black the man was ..." (100).

The narrative's dialogism balances the usual inequities and racial conflict(s) so commonly pervading Wright's narratives. The entire story deviates from the Wrightsian pattern with the presence of an African American male who is in direct contrast to the familiar characterization(s) of the transgressive male, headed toward fugitive status, awaiting the confrontational and eventual tragic end, with the white male as pursuer and executioner. As David Bradley has observed of the characters in "Big Black Good Man," the reader finds that "the worldview they symbolize is radically different . . . . Although . . . they remain types" (*Eight Men*, xxii), Bradley adds:

> The black male is no weak, confused black boy, killing a white woman before the white man accuses him of raping her; he is so big, so black and so sexually—and emotionally—capable that he can love a woman the white man thinks is a whore and can slay a white man with a verbal "drop dead" (xxii)

Eva though Lena in "Big Black Good Man" and Eva in *The Outsider* have class differences, they both have positive relationships with African American males, and their status as females in the narrative structure is elevated in contrast to Wright's other white female characters.

The story, "Big Black Good Man," appeared in *Esquire Magazine* in 1957 (Bradley) when Wright was experiencing a transformation in his fiction. The typical Wright was not selling as he had previously done in 1940 and 1945 with his two best sellers, *Native Son* and *Black Boy*. Even though *The Long Dream* has vestiges of the old Wright, it presents a different type of African male character in its imaging of Fishbelly, an only child of black middle-class status, who experiences white female challenges, even a trumped up charge of rape, but ends up being freed and leaving for Paris where "all of his bridges to the past would be destroyed" (349). A victorious and positive ending occurs in *The Long Dream* and "Big Black Good Man."

Fishbelly's story has both sameness and difference regarding the lives of most of Wright's male characters. The white oppression in *The Long Dream* is overt, as in other Wright texts, yet the relationship that Fishbelly and his father have with the corrupt white policeman regarding the checks deviates from the Wrightsian formula. Wright elevates his main characters socioeconomically in the narrative process despite the traditional antics of racist and corrupt characters, like Cantley and his cronies, who intimidate poor, subservient, and frightened African Americans. The symbols of white oppression, so numerous in Wright's texts, become a white shark, white snow, white picket fences, white faces, voices, and most notably the white female. However, the frequent utilization of the dangerous white female character paired with the naïve, unsuspecting or suspecting African American male victim has provoked a range of critical responses either sympathetic or oppositional to Wright's political and social intent.

As noted earlier, perhaps the most strident criticism is that of Neal A. Lester's most recent argument regarding Wright's use of the African American male and white female to expose white racism in America. Lester's analysis of the situation of Saul, the African American male protagonist in "The Man Who Killed a Shadow," offers another interpretation of how Wright presents the African American male and white female relationship in his narratives. Lester argues that the mythology of the black male as rapist is perpetuated by Saul's actions in Wright's story and by the lyrics of gangster rappers. He states:

> The peculiar conditions of American race relations have spawned myths and folklore that intertwine race, gender, sexuality and violence. Richard Wright's "The Man Who Killed a Shadow," in his collection *Eight Men* (1940), complicates this interconnectedness of sexuality, violence, gender, and race, showing that for the central character, Saul Sanders, myth and reality are one and the same.

NOTES

1   Neal A. Lester's article on Wright's short story, "The Man Who Killed a Shadow,"
     in the *Richard Wright Newsletter*, analyzes the phallogocentrism of some gangster
     rap music, which glorifies the sexual aggression and sexual violence of African
     American males. Lester argues that this warped treatment of male and female
     sexuality pervading so much of the music can be observed in Wright's narrative
     in the situation of the African American male janitor and the white female
     librarian.

CHAPTER 4

Sexual Diversity In Wright's Characterization Of Bigger Thomas: Homosocialism, Homoeroticism, And The Feminine

Richard Wright's most treasured, captivating, provocative, and timeless character in all of his fiction is none other than Bigger Thomas, the protagonist in his bestseller and major literary achievement, *Native Son*. When one reads the Wright canon, particularly his fiction and autobiographies, one can easily discern that Wright is Bigger and Bigger is Wright. Through Bigger, Wright initiated a scathing voice of protest against a society that created, cultivated, and perpetuated racial conflict, violence, and injustice against African Americans. It was solely Wright's fiction that created the paradigm, the premise from which successive African American writers, especially those of the 60s, express themselves. Earning the title of the Father of the Black Protest Novel with *Native Son*, Wright's Bigger has garnered a place in history as the prototype, the archetype, of the angry, rebellious, disenfranchised, dispossessed, militant, and even revolutionary African American male, who feels so strongly victimized by a racially divided American society that historically has targeted African American males via lynching, police brutality, and, in most recent years, racial profiling.

Most of Wright's fiction is grounded in the victimization of African American males. His first literary achievement, a collection of short fiction, *Uncle Tom's Children* (1938), could specifically be titled *Uncle Tom's Sons* since every protagonist is a male who is victimized by whites, is often killed, and prevails as a tragic hero. In fact, most of Wright's fictional texts have male signifiers in their titles or male protagonists in their narratives: *Native Son* (1940), *The Outsider* (1953), *Savage Holiday* (1954), *The Long Dream* (1958), *Eight Men* (1961), *Lawd Today* (1963), and *Rite of Passage* (1994).

Prior to writing *Native Son*, Wright had already presented to American audiences a cadre of male figures. *Lawd Today*, initially entitled *Cesspool*, Wright's first novel attempt in the 1930s, but published posthumously in 1963, and *Uncle Tom's Children* provide the reader with scenarios and situations that give credence to this preoccupation with males and racialized conflict while, simultaneously, negating and diminishing female characters. By the end of *Uncle Tom's Children*, the reader has been saturated with an American society, specifically a racially divided South, that is beleaguered with the problems, challenges, and aspirations of African American people, especially the males. Also, in 1940, Wright debuts his favorite son, perhaps more comrade than son, and what Wright terms America's *native son*, Bigger Thomas. Also, Wright's depiction of Bigger elicited a body of discourse that questions this menacing image of black maleness that became so entrenched in America's literary and social history while another, perhaps more tenuous one, argues Bigger's redeeming, empathetic qualities. However, in addition to the controversial image that Bigger's characterization has suggested throughout the years, as most notably treated in James Baldwin's essay "Everybody's Protest Novel"[1] and in Wright gender and feminist criticism, the Bigger character, along with other males in Wright's fiction, presents a sexual consciousness that suggests not just sexual ambivalence, as Margaret Walker Alexander has argued, but what may be perceived as sexual complexity or sexual diversity.

Eve Sedgwick's *Between Men*, which explores a homosocial and homoerotic dynamic in English literature, offers an appropriate paradigm for examining males and male culture in Wright's fiction. Sedgwick's theory of homosocial desire, in which she cites relationships that men have with each other, is suggestive of the relationship that Wright creates with Bigger. The example of Jessie Helms and Ronald Reagan sharing the same views on family policy is analogous to the dynamics surrounding Bigger's characterization and Wright's political agenda in *Native Son*. Bigger is Wright's conduit, his creation for illumining, exposing the racial climate of 1940s America, not just in the urban north but in America in general. Because of what Sedgwick cites in a specific definition of patriarchy as an "interdependence and solidarity among men that enables them to dominate women," she asks if this "continuum between men loving men and men promoting the interests-of-men," the latter, especially, being the case of Wright and his males, would "have the same intuitive force that it has for women" (3). And it is in this context that Sedgwick proceeds to cite the homosocial and homoerotic existing in literary texts, but before doing so, she asks: "Why should the different shapes of the homosocial continuum be an interesting question? Why should it be a *literary* question" (5)? Sedgwick responds, "Its importance for the practical politics of the gay movement as a minority rights movement is already obvious from the recent history of strategic and philosophical differences between lesbians and gay men. In addition, it is theoretically interesting partly as a way of approaching a larger question of 'sexual politics': What does it mean—what difference does it make—when a social or political relationship is sexualized? If the relation of homosocial to homosexual bonds is so shifty, then what theoretical framework do we have for drawing any links between sexual and power relationships" (5)?

Richard Wright's *Native Son* can certainly be viewed as an exemplar of this link between sexual and power relationships. The link can be observed in Wright's fiction even before *Native Son's* Mary Dalton/Bigger Thomas relationship presented a mirror of the racialized sexuality phenomenon that historically existed in American society. Earlier Wright texts that present very obvious sexualized relationships, subjugated to the sociopolitical and cultural constructs of power in the larger culture, are "Big Boy Leaves Home," with Big Boy, his buddies, and Bertha, the white woman, "Long Black Song," with Sarah and the white salesman, and "Bright and Morning Star," with Johnnie-Boy and Reva, his white girlfriend. These texts are only the microcosm of the macrocosm of sexualized relationships in Wright fiction as evidenced in his later novels: *Native Son, The Outsider, The Long Dream,* and *Savage Holiday.*

It is in the context of Sedgwick's theory that one can examine the male-to-male bond that exists between the writer Wright and his most critically studied character, Bigger Thomas. Considering the corpus of Wright's art, his fiction and nonfiction, as well as the philosophical worldview that evolves from it, one can certainly discern that Bigger prevails as one character that endured—one who represents all that Wright was awed by and capable of being, had he not been "refined" with books and the literary culture. Cross Damon in Wright's existential novel, *The Outsider*, is simply a well-read, employed Bigger, given the vestiges of existentialism some critics have attributed to the Bigger character, who is sometimes viewed as one who prefigures Cross. And because of the dramatic effect and definitive presentation of Bigger's thoughts and actions that readers experience *Native Son*, one can argue that Wright is enamored of Bigger, and that a homosocial and homoerotic effect exists between Wright's male characters in *Native Son*, as cited earlier in the short story, "Big Boy Leaves Home."

A reading of *Black Boy* and Wright's most famous essay, "How 'Bigger' Was Born," which introduces the novel in its first 1940 publication, as well as other texts in the Wright corpus, can convince one that there is so much of Wright in Bigger and Bigger in Wright. This view of Wright and Bigger is shared by Margaret Walker Alexander in her biography, *Richard Wright: Deamonic Genius*, where she states, "In his creative writing process and effort, Wright and Bigger become momentarily the same; emotionally they are the same. Wright not only becomes involved with Bigger as character, he expresses his own subliminal desires, and in the creative process of transferring reality into fiction, he translates these desires into those of his character, Bigger Thomas" (148). And though Wright presents Bigger as tough, brutish, and callous, especially in his interactions with females, he also creates a male to male bond that exists not only with Wright as creator of Bigger (like the bond between Dr. Frankenstein and the monster he creates), but also a bond that exists between other males in his fiction. It is this link between males in Wright's fiction that is suggestive of Sedgwick's concept of homosocial desire and homoeroticism. The feminine Wright creates nurturing, defensive, suggestive innuendoes with his males, which reveals not just a preoccupation with them but a treatment of their bonding that engenders erotic overtones. The male character, in the case of Bigger, is so fleshed out in *Native Son*, that he becomes the center of Wright's politicized artistic consciousness. Quintessentially, Wright is Bigger and Bigger is Wright. In essence, Wright is psychologically enamored of Bigger, and this chapter will examine the dynamics of the affair between author and protagonist, as well as the homosocialism and homoeroticism that transpires in the narrative of *Native Son*. As Wright goes in and out of these different phases of sexuality, the homosocial and homoerotic connection never wanes.

In Walker Alexander's biography, she contends that Wright's successes and failures in life relate to the Greek myth of Medusa, one of the monster sisters, the Gorgons, who had serpents for her hair. To Walker Alexander, Medusa symbolizes Wright's life, his difficulties, and frustrations in his relations with women. She writes, "For Wright, a woman was an enemy, who failed to give him love and happiness by frustrating him in his search for meaning and success" (107). As stated earlier, Wright's first contact with bigotry, according to his accounts in the autobiographical *Black Boy*, was from his family, especially the females: his mother, grandmother, and aunts. Thus, according to Walker Alexander, "Medusa is also the woman in him, the capricious *feminine* self that was part of his acute sensitivity" (108). Moreover, this acute sensitivity is inclusive of his homophobia, which is also mentioned in Walker Alexander's discussion of Wright's sexuality.

When studying the life and works of Richard Wright, there are basically two schools of thought that emerge regarding his sexuality. One is that he was solely a heterosexual whose relations with women were publicly known, and if he was anything other than heterosexual, such as bisexual or homosexual, there is no evidence of it (Rowley). The other is that he was sexually ambivalent: heterosexual, but with a compelling *feminine* side, all pointing to what Walker Alexander terms "sexual conflict, confusion, and revulsion" (319).

Margaret Walker Alexander's account of an episode in New York created a shroud of suspicion regarding Wright's sexuality, and she has publicly recounted her version of the incident, revealing the estranged relationship that resulted from her New York visit and encounter with Wright in 1939. In summary, she suggests the possibility of Wright having homosexual tendencies as a result of her observing a rather revealing situation involving the writer and another male, playwright Theodore Ward. However, regardless of how one interprets this encounter the Wright biographer had in New York, her frustration was more centered on Wright's and his friends' reactions to the incident and, more important, Wright's imperative: "I think the best thing for you to do is pack your things and get out of here the first thing in the morning" (135). Apparently, Wright felt that Walker Alexander had the potential for or had already been discussing him in the context of homosexuality, which he and his literary cohorts felt would be damaging to his career; after all, *Native Son* was awaiting publication the next year, 1940.

Juxtaposed with Walker Alexander's account of the New York episode is that of another Wright biographer, Hazel Rowley, who, in *Richard Wright: The Life and Times* (2001), characterizes Walker Alexander as a talkative young girl whose "reputation for gossip was . . . firmly established" (171). While Walker Alexander's discussion points to the New York incident as an unfortunate set of circumstances, deriving from involuntary comments and remarks innocently or perhaps naively made, Rowley presents her research on the matter, which includes Walker Alexander's own admission of talking too much and confiding in people (171). In a rather acrimonious tone, Rowley further contends that the close contact observed between Wright and Ward existed because of the small size of the hotel room, which had little capacity to offer roomy accommodations for visitors (172). Some may think that Walker Alexander's inclusion of the New York incident in her repertoire of Wright scholarship may tend to preclude a purely textual approach to discussions of sexuality in his texts. However, Wright's fiction is so fecund with sexual nuances and sexual dynamics that any textual analysis of sexuality in it, whether sociocultural or poststructuralist, has the potential of unveiling a plethora of hypotheses regarding the writer's sexual consciousness. The pattern of male and female relationships and the recurrence of male homosociality, i.e., the gathering of males who formulate a discourse that is not only of racial victimization but female vilifying, as well as the homoeroticism, are fodder for sexual inferences. Thus, evident in Wright's fiction and even nonfiction (*Black Power*) is an artistic consciousness permeated with sexual complexity or diversity: male bonding or homosocialism, homoeroticism, and misogyny, all intertwined with heterosexuality.

After publishing *Uncle Tom's Children*, Wright vowed he would never write another tale to make bankers' daughters weep; he knew that American audiences needed another type of African American male to put before them, to "wake them up" (the alarm clock at beginning of the novel) and to dangle before them (the rat scene). Moreover, because of his experiences and observations as a youth in the early South, he wrote the essay, "How 'Bigger' Thomas Was Born." And regardless of the varied levels of Wright's thought, i.e., the intellectual, philosophical, humanitarian, etc., at the core of the writer's persona is the revolutionary, the angry, the rebellious, or as Walker Alexander has suggested, the demonic Wright, his Biggerism.

Perhaps it is Wright's obvious effect of misogyny and sexism in his works that imply an ambivalent, complex sexual consciousness. As one follows Wright's path of female exploitative subjugation, and even deaths of female characters, one also becomes aware of not only their inequality with male characters but also the special and extensive relationship the males acquire with Wright throughout his narratives. In the case of Bigger, of whom, as I suggested earlier, Wright is "psychologically enamored" (despite their vast differences in background and intellectual sophistication), we see in Bigger's hatred of whites Wright's own disdain for the Euroamerican mindset as a result of European colonialism and the enslavement of his African ancestors. Bigger's feminization, his impotence, develops because he is deemed by the larger culture as a failure, but his self fulfillment and empowerment occur as a result of killing Mary, the white male patriarchy's most prized possession, the white woman. Moreover, according to Wright, Bigger's act of murder is an act of creation. Thus, Wright's literary success comes in the killing of not simply the symbol of white purity and power, the white Mary Dalton, notwithstanding the murder of her African American counterpart, Bessie Mears, but also the killing of the underestimation of the black criminal mind, which fascinated Wright from the observation of some

African American males in childhood and from his reading of Dostoyevsky and the existentialist writers in adulthood. Through Bigger's voice and his actions, Wright's desires, he is able to reconstruct his worth in the eyes of whites, to whom his fiction is primarily aimed. Yet, ironically, he must literally kill the blackness—kill Bigger—to achieve his goal; for Wright's literary success, a cadre of African American males and females become the sacrificial lamb, attesting to the sadomasochism often associated with Wright and Bigger in *Native Son*.

Wright's essay, "How Bigger Was Born," creates the context for understanding the conceptualization and evolution of the character Bigger Thomas in the fictional *Native Son*. Bigger's desires are Wright's desires, and from Wright's sociopolitical worldview vis a vis his protagonist, the reader recognizes an intimacy between author and subject that is uniquely profound in African American literary history. Between *Uncle Tom's Children* and *Black Boy*, Wright's Bigger, like his other African American males, rises from the heap of ashes, like the mythological Phoenix, to make declarations that reading audiences had yet to encounter in 1940. Houston Baker's assertion, "... it is impossible to understand the aspirations, turnings, and contradictions of his work without some understanding of his life" (122), points to a substantive link between the autobiographical Wright and the fiction of the author. In this testimonial ("How 'Bigger' Was Born") on how the character became imprinted on the mind of his creator, the reader is apprised of Bigger as the writer's response to the racial landscape of America—a landscape he articulated in poems, essays, and short fiction even before the publication of *Native Son*. Thus, Bigger, from the outset, becomes a major artistic agent for Wright's sociopolitical discourse; Bigger's voice resonates in all of Wright's fiction. But along with this politicized Bigger is the sexualized one, and there are several areas in the novel that present Wright's intimacy with Bigger—presenting homosocial, homoerotic, and heterosexual behaviors, all of them culminating in Wright's perennial misogyny and the creation of this feminine self: the homosocialism, the forcing of the knife lick with Gus, the homoeroticism, and the plethora of antifemale episodes in the narrative.

One of the initial scenarios that presents the homosocial—i., e., men promoting the *interests* of men—is the male-to-male bonding that occurs with Bigger and his buddies, Jack, Gus, and G.H. The cajoling, the situations of camaraderie and fellowship they all share with each other are reminiscent of Big Boy and his friends in "Big Boy Leaves Home." As in "Big Boy," there are four buddies who comprise the so-called gang in *Native Son.* Just as Blythe and Sweet have observed the homosocial yielding to the homoerotic in "Big Boy" (chapter 2), so is this same dynamic observed in *Native Son.*

The gathering of males inside and outside the poolroom to discuss the robbing of Blum's store includes moments they share of mockery, laughter, awe, and fear. Bigger's disposition moves from critiquing, menacing behavior to what Wright terms as "childlike wonder" (16). In response to the billboard Bigger sees of the State Attorney, Buckley, whose words of warning to urban youth is, "You Can't Win," Bigger retorts, astutely, "You let whoever pays you off win" (13)! In response to a plane flying overhead, Bigger states, "Looks like a little bird" (16). Moreover, Bigger's fear in the first section of the novel labeled Fear includes role playing, mood swings, and threatening behavior that eventually climaxes in a brutish, sadistic gesture, suggestive of homoeroticism and sodomy.

The knife scene with Gus is often critically interpreted as an act of cowardice, but it can also be perceived as homoerotic. In describing Bigger's threatening act, Wright states, "Bigger held the open blade an inch from Gus's lips. 'Lick it,' Bigger said, his body tingling with elation" (39). The tingling elation and hand-held knife, a phallic symbol, occurs within the context of this continuum of male companionship that weaves in and out of Wright's fiction, as examined earlier. There are other inferences readers may have other than the dynamics of thuggish, criminal behavior, and one is that repressed anger "swells" and expresses itself in a tingling, aggressive gesture of sensual dimensions.

This scene continues with Wright's description of Gus's subjugation by Bigger. Prior to the knife scene, Gus is physically attacked by Bigger, "The muscles of his body gave a tightening lunge and he saw his fist come down on the side of Gus's head; he had struck him really before he was conscious of doing so" (38). Gus falls to his knees, and this physical attack proceeds with choking. Afterwards, Gus actually is forced to lick the knife, "Gus's lips moved toward the knife; he stuck out his tongue and touched the blade" (39). As tears stream down Gus's lips, Bigger gives further orders for Gus to put his hands up and continues to use the knife to make physical contact with Gus, "He put the tip of the blade into Gus's shirt and then made an arc with his arm, as though cutting a circle" (39). In essence, and in the street vernacular, Bigger has made Gus his *bitch* in the midst of the epitome of the male, macho environ—a poolroom. Also, Bigger has "screwed" Gus, whose fate ends with him "flying through the rear door" (40) of the poolroom, as a result of Bigger's last and final attack.

Bigger has dramatically feminized Gus. However, juxtaposed with Gus's feminization is that of Bigger. When Bigger further vents his anger by cutting Doc's pool table with the knife, the poolroom owner gets his gun, another phallic symbol, and spews, "Get out before I shoot you!" (41). Wright comments, "Doc was angry and Bigger was afraid" (41). Doc has now subjugated and victimized Bigger. Is Bigger also feminized now? If the rest of the gang only realized how scared he was, in gang terms Bigger would be considered a female, in gang vernacular, a *bitch*.

The feminization of Bigger continues to develop even as the reader observes those aspects of the novel that are homosocial, antifemale, and suggest the homoerotic, as well as the feminine. First, there is the litany of chastisements that come from Mrs. Thomas, whose denigrating comments are leveled at Bigger, who has yet to be a resourceful and valued family member. After all, Bigger is a nineteen year old dropout who spends most of his time with his gang buddies. The accusatory verbiage that comes from Bigger's mother points to the conflicting relations of mother and son. Mrs. Thomas exclaims, "Bigger sometimes I wonder why I birthed you"; "We wouldn't have to live in this garbage dump if you had any manhood in you" (8); and, finally, "Bigger, honest, you the most no-countest man I ever seen in all my life" (9). To this last assailment, Bigger responds, "You done told me that a thousand times" (9). Bigger has inherited the role of male protector and provider in a household of females and younger siblings who are dependent upon him for their own survival. However, because he is not able to provide for them as needed, he feels impotent. In his thoughts, "He hated his family because he knew that they were suffering and that he was powerless to help them" (10). Moreover, Mrs. Thomas's comments exacerbate this impotence that he is continuously struggling with, trying to break through, to find some semblance of self confidence for his manhood.

Bigger's emasculation occurs early in the narrative, creating a dichotomous characterization of him—the masculine and the feminine. One aspect of Bigger's character demonstrates strength, aggression, and intimidating behavior, e.g., the killing of the rat, talking back to his mother and his siblings, and of course, threatening Gus with the knife. However, another aspect of Bigger's behavior is that of fear and doubt, which is masked by this aggression. And it is this fearful and doubtful aspect of his personality that engenders the feminine.

Bigger enters a homosocial world when he is with the gang. They role play, mimicking rich white moguls, and discuss the robbing of Blum's store while playing pool. It continues when they decide to go to the movies and are viewing and commenting on the lives and sexuality of rich white people. In his introduction to a revised edition of *Native Son* (1998), Arnold Rampersad reports on Wright's first manuscript submission in which the writer included one episode in the movie scene that he was required to cut for the 1940 Book-of-the-Month publication: the masturbation scene with Bigger and Jack (xviii). In this unabridged version, Wright gives an overt description of Bigger's and Jack's interplay while they are jokingly masturbating before the movie begins. Wright also includes a use of the double entendre in street language as Jack and Bigger are doing what they call "polishing my nightstick" (30). This homosocial event develops into a homoerotic one even before the movie begins with the presence of a woman on screen—a white female they mock and, simultaneously, desire. While they sit "listening to the pipe organ playing low and soft" (30), Wright images the boys' interplay with a type of crescendo dramatic effect, culminating in a language of orgasm: "You gone?," "You pull off fast," and "I'm gone. . . . God . . . damn . . ." (30). Jack and Bigger, who anticipate their heterosexual experiences, "I wished I had Bessie here now" (30), are having self-sex within the close quarters of the movie house, which is akin to the close quarters of their cramped living quarters where privacy is encroached upon by the presence of other family members. In addition, by having self-sex together, they are having sex vicariously with each other.

Wright creates another situation involving Bigger's sexuality that points to the larger socioeconomic constructs controlling his life; depressed, urban living conditions have an influence on his sexuality. Ralph Ellison's "Trueblood" chapter, which treats incest among the rural poor, is another exemplar of this phenomenon since father, daughter, and wife are compelled to sleep in the same bed because of their poverty and close quarters. In addition, Jack's and Bigger's masturbating "competition," involving who will finish first, seems more important to them than the absent Other—the female.

The masturbation scene is followed with mocking statements Bigger and friends make about the lives of rich whites. When Bigger views on the screen "the rich young woman . . . laughing and dancing with her lover," he states, "I'd like to be there" (32). But that desire is ridiculed by his buddies, and though Bigger expresses the desire to be like the couple he sees on the screen, he is reminded of the futility of having such delusions of grandeur by the language of his peers, who poke fun at his looks and his esteemed sense of self. Of course, guffaws follow when Bigger expresses the desire to be a part of the white world, but such commenting and laughter indicate their ability to mock and ridicule the very elements of society that can be painful reminders of their socially and economically deprived lives, their impotence.

Wright is also using signifying to mock the stereotypical perception of African American males by whites—the gorilla image that Jack associates with Bigger in the movies anticipates the ape-like image attributed to Bigger by whites later in the novel. By ridiculing themselves, Bigger and his buddies are demonstrating, again, what Michael Best has formulated as black male agency and resistance. The homosocialism in the movie scene, as well as the role-playing on the street corner where Bigger and Gus verbally impersonate J. P. Morgan and the President of the United States in a telephone conversation, is definitely an empowering event. It provides Bigger and his buddies the autonomy and license to resist and respond to socioeconomic inequalities in their communities and lives. However, the seriousness of their condition does not go unaddressed, for Wright has Gus respond to Bigger's ambition when he observes the plane flying overhead: "If you wasn't black and if you had some money and if they'd let you go to that aviation school, you could fly a plane" (17). This comment, like others interspersed throughout the narrative, points to just one of Wright's myriad desires— to put before his reading audience the possibilities of achievement that often escape the Biggers of America.

Moreover, just as Bigger wishes to fly planes like the ones he sees flying overhead, he wishes to have a lifestyle like rich whites. However, the subtext of his friends' response is because he is black, poor, and unattractive, reminding them of a gorilla, he does not belong to that group; he belongs where he is, with them. Thus, when Bigger is commenting on the plane flying overhead, he is reminded of how excluded he is from the American dream. When Bigger tries to identify with power—whiteness, richness, and white women—his desires are cut off, shut down, and he is reminded of his impotence—his powerlessness—in a capitalist, racialized society that historically has created the poverty, joblessness, and slum conditions he must endure. It is these parts of the text that are often cited as Wright's propagandist trajectories: Wright inculcating his desires into the thoughts of his protagonist. Expressing the writer's own political sentiments, Bigger states wistfully in speaking of whites, "They get a chance to do everything" (16). The situation of Bigger and Mary's relationship in the narrative, as well as black male/white female relationships in Wright's other fiction, is Wright's emphasis on the African American male's desire of the white female even though he is forbidden to be attracted to her and will be violently punished if he has that desire and acts on it. This theme resonates throughout twentieth century American literature, especially African American, and Wright lived long enough to see it resonate in other African American fictional texts, such as *Invisible Man's* chapter, "The Battle Royale," as well as his own, *The Long Dream.*

The dialogue of Bigger and buddies in the movie scene presents not only their version of social and economic inequalities but also their economic impotency and their own exhortations of sexual prowess, which makes the female a crucial subject for this discourse. This covert critiquing of economic injustice is also another example of Wright's "refracted voice," his Marxist voice, expressing his desires vis a vis Bigger and his buddies. It is a factor that is evidenced in the entire narrative of *Native Son*, but it is nonetheless rendered through male homosocialism when the males are awed at the wealth displayed by the images and actions on the screen while they make exclamations of their sexual prowess with the white female. The phallic-centeredness of their comments not only reflects the phallogocentrism of this male group's thinking and Wright's text, but also it presents a dialectic of social and sexual stereotyping of both black and white worlds. Their own sexual touting and the comments they make concerning the deviant behavior of whites not only illustrate their combative and innovative techniques for resisting the white world they, generally, vicariously encounter, but they also mock themselves. Critiquing, as well as soliciting, takes the form of the following statements aimed at Bigger concerning the white female:

> "Ah, them rich white women'll go to bed with anybody
> from a poodle on up. They even have their chauffeurs.
> say, . . . if you run across anything too much for you to you
> to handle at that place, let me know." (33)

The comments that Bigger and his buddies make regarding "rich white folks" and the white female is their way of critiquing this particular class and the historical phenomenon of racism that has contributed to their bleak existence. While they suggest the bestiality of the white female, "Ah, man, them rich white women'll go to bed with anybody, from a poodle on up," and the comment that follows, "they even have their chauffeurs" (33), might suggest an equating of African American males with animals. If white females go to bed with what is deemed as inappropriate and abhorred animals, then they will go to bed with African American men. Since their comments are couched in a mocking and ridiculing mode, the deprivation of their own lives, though implied, is not overtly addressed. In fact, even though there exists a chasm between their world and the world they view on screen, signifying such attests to their ability to cope regardless of their stark reality: "They are rich and we are poor."

The shared deprivation of Bigger and his buddies has provided the impetus for plotting the Blum robbery, and to them it is an act of empowerment. Other shared experiences are just as empowering. Though Wright presents the resulting complexities of enslavement and a segregated society, i.e., poor housing, unemployment, and poor educational opportunities, the bonding dynamics of Bigger and his buddies, their homosocialism, mockingly address those inequities, and the discourse that emanates from them represents their critique of American society's historically racist and capitalist posture. Like Big Boy and his buddies, Bigger and his gang resort to signifying and innovatively (like Big Boy's "quall") perform role-playing as a coping strategy to respond to racial injustice and economic deprivation. His killing of white Mary Dalton is symbolically viewed as his subconscious resistance to white racism; however, at the beginning of *Native Son*, a conscious and yet covert way of striking back at these adversaries is his participation in gang-like activities. By belonging to a gang, Bigger, like so many urban youths, especially African American, achieves a communal identity in a sprawling urban section of Chicago, the South side, where familial and other institutions of care giving can often be ineffective. The role-playing and, especially, the movie episode provide an environment for homoerotic "gestures" and homosocial activities that primarily create a discourse of signifying; Bigger and his buddies use every opportunity to mock white life and sexuality. It is their combative response to the larger society, and it ensures their ability to cope and survive.

Bigger's feelings of bitterness toward whites becomes more defined when he first encounters Mary and Jan. After being wedged between them in the car he is employed to drive for the Daltons, Wright informs the reader of his thoughts, "Bigger felt trapped . . . he distrusted them, really hated them" (71). This is one of a series of entrapments in *Native Son* that critics have noted, and in the car scene, Wright clearly establishes Bigger's feelings of hate toward Mary from the moment he meets her, to the moments of her drunken stupor, and, finally, to the moments of her death and dismemberment via decapitation. Even though Mary has befriended Bigger, he thinks, "But for all of that, she was white and he hated her" (81). Subsequently, Mary's death becomes the catalyst for the plot's development, its raison d' etre, yet the horror of her death is exacerbated by her decapitation—again, Wright's gothic touch, coupled with antifemaleness. However, her decapitation is necessary for her cremation, and her total destruction is not consummated until she is burned.

Readers may recall that Wright's pyromania originates as a child according to his *Black Boy* account of a fire that causes him to nearly burn down his grandmother's house and their only shelter at the time. Moreover, the decapitation and burning of the female body reflect Wright's Freudian, analytical psychology influence; the male's act of destroying femaleness is symbolic of destroying the power and control females have over males even before they enter into other systems of control in society. Such power often associated with females exists because of their ability to not only biologically continue the development of human beings but also prevail in this process of development during the period of nurturing their offspring. In Wright's fiction, the antifemale behavior usually proceeds from either a homosocial or heterosexual situation. After Bigger has had invigorating and challenging moments with his buddies, a homosocial experience, there are antics of hate directed toward females.

In addition, the reader observes Bigger's relations with other males, this homosocialism, as well as with females, his heterosexualism, and it is the latter that leads to acts of unadulterated antifemale behavior. By the time Bigger puts Mary to bed, she has aggravated and annoyed him with her gestures and questions—her liberal innuendoes. Her drunkenness in the car becomes another facet of her aggravating behavior that causes discomfort for Bigger, just as her suggestion for them to go to the chicken place causes him embarrassment and anxiety, especially when his girlfriend, Bessie sees him with two white strangers, Jan and, of course, Mary. Bigger's heterosexual moments proceed from this aggravating disposition, for when he has to assist her in her drunken stupor, he thinks, "in spite of his hate for her, he was excited standing there watching her like this" (82). As he is trying to get her to her bedroom and, simultaneously, avoid detection (for his sake especially), readers are informed of Bigger's desire of Mary in Wright's description:

He eased his hand, the fingers spread wide, up the center of her back and her face came toward him and her lips touched his, like something he had imagined. He stood her on her feet and she swayed against him. He tightened his arms as his lips pressed tightly against hers and he felt her body moving strongly. The thought and conviction that Jan had had her a lot flashed through his mind. He kissed her again and felt the sharp bones of her hips move in a hard and veritable grind. Her mouth was open and her breath came slow and deep.

. . . . He tightened his fingers on her breast, kissing her again, feeling her move toward him. (84-85)

Related to this scene are Rampersad's comments on an earlier scene that was cut from the original manuscript, which has Bigger responding "sexually to a newsreel that shows Mary and apparently other wealthy, carefree young white women cavorting on a beach in Florida" (xviii). His editors later cut it from the 1940 publication because it presents Mary as a sensuous female, an image that would offend whites. Nonetheless, this moment of intimacy and intenseness Bigger has with Mary is "cut off" by the intrusion of a blind Mrs. Dalton, thus causing Bigger's justifiable fear— being entrapped clandestinely in the bedroom of a white female. Wright has created a heterosexual situation that is immediately aborted and politicized by the entrance of Mrs. Dalton, another female, and Wright has once again reminded his readers of the black male/white female taboo, and Bigger's opportunity to express his heterosexuality is thwarted.

Wright reiterates Bigger's heterosexuality with the relationship he has with Bessie Mears, his girlfriend, who is introduced in the same context as Bigger's mother. Also, like Mary, Bessie is immediately established as an annoying, even menacing character very early in the narrative when Bigger is forced to accompany Jan and Mary to the chicken shack where she works. Bigger's presence with two white strangers in a black joint on the Southside of Chicago, of course, creates suspicion because of Jim Crowism and the potential the scenario has for creating a chasm between not only Bigger and his girlfriend but between him and the African American community. Wright continues with this pattern of using white characters to create tension not only between whites and African Americans but also among African American themselves, most notably in such texts as "Down by the Riverside," *The Outsider, The Long Dream*, and even *Native Son*. Because of the violent vigilantism that occurs with Blacks in Chicago after Bigger is pursued for the murder of Mary, the African American community is upset with him, voicing their blame of Bigger for their victimization by white terrorism. One Southside resident spouts, "The papers say they beatin' us up all over the city. They don't care whut black man they git. We's all dogs in they sight!" In addition, the revolutionary Wright comes forth as he has the character continue with, "Yuh gotta stan' up 'n' fight these folks" (251).

Moreover, Wright's characterization of Bessie is such that she becomes one of the most devalued characters in the text. Race, class, and gender issues come to the fore with Bessie because of her depiction as an alcoholic African American domestic, who earns little, lives in poverty, and recognizes the bleakness of her existence and, especially, danger with Bigger as a fugitive murderer. Bessie's remarks reflect her hopelessness, "Bigger, please! Don't do this to me! Please! All I do is work, work like a dog! From morning till night. I ain't got no happiness" (180). Her status as a commodity is realized in the manner in which she is treated by whites and Bigger, with his actions of rape and murder reducing her to nothingness, like the murder and dismemberment of Mary. Readers become cognizant of the status of both females; whether rich or poor, their lives are dispensable, for Wright emphasizes his antifemaleness with both characters being the objects of Bigger's gruesome acts of violence.

Some critics have never understood the necessity of Bessie's murder. Even Wright's friend, Jane Newton, who is reported to have offered suggestions regarding Mary Dalton's dismemberment, was horrified about Wright's decision to kill Bessie (Rowley 155). Rowley gives the following account:

> One afternoon in midsummer, Wright came into the
> kitchen, flopped down in a chair, and said: "Jane, I'm

going to kill Bessie." Jane was horrified. "Oh no, Dick!"
she thought it unnecessary in terms of the plot. Nor did
she think it would shed new light on Bigger's character.
But Wright had decided that the novel had reached a point
where something exciting or violent had to happen . . . . "I
gotta kill her . . . she's gotta go." (155)

As noted earlier, when Bigger kills Bessie by smashing her head with a
brick to prevent what he perceives as her disclosure of his murder of Mary,
readers are exposed to another realm of Wright horror. Just as the murder
of Mary is followed by dismemberment, the murder of Bessie results in
her body's disposal down the air shaft. Of course, Wright's and Bigger's
vehemence do not end with the smashed head; readers eventually are
informed that Bessie died of exposure as a result of still being alive when
Bigger disposes of her body. Wright compounds one act of horror with
another. Bessie's death, like that of Mary, proceeds from a heterosexual
experience even though the sexual act she shares with Bigger is a
nonconsensual one. Perhaps it is more rape than a nonconsensual sex act,
given the details surrounding it, but because of her race and the historical,
social, and political context in which Wright is writing, Mary's death, as
noted earlier, is viewed as more rape than murder while Bessie's rape or
nonconsensual act becomes more murder than rape or sexual violation.
Moreover, since much of the gender/feminist criticism on *Native Son* finds
no substantive reason for Bessie's murder, it seems that Wright utilizes it as
a way of exacerbating not only Bigger's criminality but his own antifemale
stance in his fiction.

Thus, heterosexuality in *Native Son* as in most of Wright's fiction, is
hardly ever a positive erotic and pleasurable experience; it is accompanied
with frustration, anxiety, and conflict. There is hardly any account of
a relaxed, pleasurable sexual experience that is void of conflict, such as
with Sarah and the salesman in "Long Black Song," Cross Damon and the
prostitute, in *The Outsider*, Fishbelly's sexual developments in *The Long
Dream*, Erskine Fowler and Mabel in *Savage Holiday*, and, of course, *Native
Son*. In fact, even though Cross and Eva prevail as the most sensuous couple

in Wright's fiction, they never consummate their relationship, and Eva's suicide precludes any hope for their union.

Given the context of a discussion of how Wright's complex, diverse sexual consciousness is evidenced in his fiction, Wright's short story, "Man of All Work," can certainly pique one's interest in how effeminacy and the infusion of a projected feminine self of Wright fictionally come to fruition. Having his male protagonist cross dress, i.e., utilize transvestitism in order to save his family from financial ruin, Wright demonstrates how he will innovatively use black masculinity to achieve his ultimate artistic goal. The protagonist, Carl Owens, dresses in his wife's clothes to secure a job as an African American female domestic in order to survive and overcome his personal challenge(s). In this particular case, Wright has created a tragic comedy that prevails as more slapstick than serious fiction with sophisticated humorous elements. However, this replacement of the male persona with a female mask, or this act of *masking maleness*, does not preclude Wright's pattern of "staging" more than "developing" dramatic conflict in this short narrative. Carl, the female-dressed male, ends up having to assist in bathing his naked white female employer, along with having to fend off sexual advances that have been aggressively made to him/her by his employer's husband. Again, Wright traps his victim, violence occurs, but, surprisingly, unlike most situations in Wright's fiction, the story has a happy ending. This short fictional narrative and *Native Son* give credence to Wright's use of varied uses of sexuality to accomplish the ultimate truth of his art—to once again confront America with a myriad of experiences African Americans often undergo in order to cope and survive the dehumanizing and oppressing elements that may confront them in a historically racially divided society. Bigger kills for survival, Cross Damon, too, as well as feigns his identity, and, thus, Carl Owens feigns femaleness. Thus, "Man of All Work" reveals how Wright will go to any extreme(s) with his characters to fulfill his mission as a writer.

Finally, regardless of the critical approach one uses to examine the fiction of Richard Wright, issues of gender, whether male or female, are germane to interpreting his texts. In the latter part of the twentieth century, practically every critical, theoretical approach has been used to comment on how Wright treats the female character while presenting to his reading audiences the overt, caustic message regarding a myriad of injustices that historically persons of African descent, particularly males, have inherited from the systems of European colonialism and American enslavement. As indicated, one would be hard pressed to deny Wright's sexism and misogyny. His consistency in critiquing white males as the major harbingers and controllers of racialized oppression and his concentration of harsh, diminishing treatments of not just African American females, but white females as well, leave him with only one other agent to demonstrate humanitarianism in his writings. In Wright's case, it is African American males; they are his first priority on the gender scale for exposing injustice; his fiction espouses this. Yet the female character is the most vital agent for leading the reader to the male. When Eve Sedgwick asks, "Why should the different shapes of the homosocial continuum be an interesting question," Richard Wright's fiction is the answer to such an inquiry. It is posited for an examination of it in terms of the "different shapes" of sexuality. The homosocialism, homoeroticism, heterosexuality, as well as a feminine self, create Richard Wright's sexual consciousness, his sexual diversity, with Bigger Thomas prevailing as his major artistic accomplishment and his most treasured fictional companion.

NOTES

1   James Baldwin's essay is an indictment of Wright's use of social protest in *Native Son*, which he feels perpetuates the stereotypes the writer wished to destroy. Baldwin equates *Native Son* to Harriet Beecher Stowe's *Uncle Tom's Cabin*. However, he later recanted his position and presented a more empathetic understanding of Wright's artistic purpose in another essay, "Alas Poor Richard."

WORKS CITED

Bahktin, M. M. *The Dialogic Imagination.* Austin: U of Texas P, 1988.

Baker, Houston. "Racial Wisdom and Richard Wright's Native Son." *Long Black Song: Essays in Black American Literature and Culture.* Charlottesville: U of Virginia P, 1972. 122-141.

Baldwin, James. "Everybody's Protest Novel." Eds. Richard Barksdale and Keneth Kinnamon. 725-729.

Barksdale, Richard, and Keneth Kinnamon, eds. *Black Writers of America: A Comprehensive Anthology.* New York: Macmillan, 1972.

Best, Stephen Michael. "Stand by Your Man: Lynch Pedagogy, and Rethinking Black Male Agency." *Representing Black Men.* Eds. Marcellus Blount, and George P. Cunningham. New York: Routledge, 1996.

Blythe, Hal, and Charlie Sweet. "Yo Mama Don Wear No Drawers: Suspended Sexuality in 'Big Boy Leaves Home.'" *Notes on Mississippi Writers* 21.1 (1989): 33-36.

Bradley, David. Preface. *12 Million Black Voices.* By Richard Wright. New York: Thunders Mouth, 1988. v-xvii.

Brown, Claude. *Manchild in the Promise Land.* New York: Simon, 1993.

Bryant, Earle. "Sexual Initiation and Survival in Richard Wright's The Long Dream." Southern Quarterly 21.3 (Spring 1983): 57-66.

Carby Hazel. *Race Men.* Cambridge: Harvard U P, 1998.

Chodorow, Nancy. *The Reproduction of Mothering: Psychoanalysis and the Sociology of Gender.* Berkeley: U of California P, 1978.

Davis, Jane. "More Force Than Human: Richard Wright's Female Characters." *Obsidian II* 1.3 (1986): 68-63.

Decosta Willis, Miriam. "Avenging Angels and Mute Mothers: Black Southern Women in Richard Wright's Fictional World." *Callaloo* 9.3 (1986): 540-544.

Early, Gerald. Afterword. *Savage Holiday.* By Richard Wright. Jackson: U of Mississippi P, 1994. 223-235.

Fetterley, Judith. *The Resisting Reader: A Feminist Approach to American Fiction.* Bloomington: Indiana UP, 1978.

Fiedler, Leslie. *Love and Death and the American Novel.* New York: Criterion, 1960.

France, Alan W. "Misogyny and Appropriation in Wright's Native Son." *Modern Fiction Studies* 34.3 (1988) 413-23.

Gates, Henry Louis, Jr. "The Blackness of Blackness: A Critique of the Sign and the Signifying Monkey." *Black Literature and Literary Theory.* Ed. Henry Louis Gates, Jr. New York: Rougledge, 1990. 295-321.

Graham. Maryemma. Introduction. *The Outsider.* By Richard Wright. New York: HarperCollins, 1993. xi-xxix.

Girard, Rene. *Deceit, Desire, and the Novel.* Baltimore: Johns Hopkins Press, 1965.

Griener, Donald J. *Women Enter the Wilderness: Male Bonding and the American Novel of the 1980s.* Columbia: U of South P, 1991.

Hine, Darlene Clark, and Ernestine Jenkins, eds. *A Question of Manhood: A Reader in U. S. Black Man's History and Masculinity.* 2 vols. Bloomington: Indiana U P, 2001.

Irving, Washington. "Rip Van Winkle." Eds. Bradley, et al. *The American Tradition in Literature.* 5th ed. New York: Random House, 1981. 235-251.

JanMohamed, Abdul R. "Sexuality On/Off the Racial Border: Foucault, Wright, and the Articulation of Racialized Sexuality." *Discourse of Sexuality: From Aristotle to Aids.* Ed. Donna C. Stanton. Ann Arbor: U of Michigan P, 1991. 94-116.

Joyce, Joyce Ann. *Richard Wright's Art of Tragedy.* Iowa City: U of Iowa P, 1986.

Keady, Sylvia H. "Richard Wright's Women Characters and Inequality." *Black American Literature Forum.* (Winter 1976): 124-28.

Lester, Neal A. "Beyond Bitches and Hoes: Sexual Violence, Violent Sex, and Sexual Fantasy in Richard Wright's 'The Man Who Killed a Shadow.'" *Richard Wright Newsletter* 8.2 (2001): 1-12.

Rampersad. Arnold. Foreword. *Lawd Today.* By Richard Wright, Boston: Northeastern U P, 1986. 1-6.

_____. Introduction. *Native Son.* By Richard Wright, New York: HarperPerrenial, (1940), 1998. ix-xxii.

_____. Afterword. *Rite of Passage.* By Richard Wright. New York: HarperCollins, 1994. 117-143.

Rowley, Hazel. *Richard Wright: The Life and the Times.* New York: Henry Holt, 2001.

Sedgwick, Eve Ksofsky. *Between Men: English Literature and Male Homosocial Desire.* New York: Colombia U P, 1985.

Walker, Alice. *In Search of Our Mothers' Gardens.* New York: Harcourt Brace, 1983.

Walker, Margaret. *Richard Wright: Daemonic Genius.* New York: Amistad, 1988.

Warren, Nagueyalti. "Black Girls and Native Sons: Female Images in Selected Works by Richard Wright." *Richard Wright: Myths and Realities.* Ed. James C. Trotman. New York: Garland, 1988. 59-77.

Wiegman, Robyn. "The Anatomy of Lynching." *A Question of Manhood: A Reader in U. S. Black Man's History and Masculinity.* Eds. Hine and Jenkins. 349-369.

Williams, Sherley Anne. "Papa Dick and Sister-Woman: Reflections on Women in the Criticism." *American Novelists Revisited: Essays in Feminist Criticism.* Ed. Fritz Fleischmann. Boston: G. K. Hall, 1982. 394-415.

_____. "Some Implications of Womanist Theory." *Reading Black, Reading Feminist.* Ed. Henry Louis Gates, Jr. New York: Meridian, 1990. 68-75.

Wright, Richard. *Black Boy.* New York: HarperCollins, 1993.

_____. *Early Works: Lawd Today, Uncle Tom's Children, Native Son.* New York: HarperCollins, 1991.

_____. "How 'Bigger' Was Born." *Native Son*. By Wright. New York: HarperPerennial (1940), 1998. 433-462.

_____. *Lawd Today*. Ann Arbor: Northeastern U P, 1986.

_____. *The Long Dream*. New York: Harper, 1987.

_____. *Native Son*. New York: HarperPerennial (1940), 1998.

_____. *The Outsider*. New York: Harper, 1993.

_____. *Rite of Passage*. New York: Harper, 1994.

_____. *Savage Holiday*. Jackson: U of Mississippi P, 1994.

APPENDIX

In *Richard Wright: Daemonic Genius*, Margaret Walker Alexander comments on how American readers responded to *Native Son's* publication in 1940. Poet and critic Sterling Brown reviewed the novel and wrote, "It is discussed by literary critics, scholars, social workers, journalists, and writers to the editor, preachers, students, and the man in the street. It seems important to the reviewer that debates on *Native Son* may be heard in grills and 'juke joints' as well as at 'literary' parties, in the deep South as well as in Chicago, among people who have not bothered much to read novels since *Ivanhoe* was assigned in high school English" (qtd. in Walker Alexander 152). Also, in numerous discussions on Richard Wright I have had with the prominent Wright scholar, Dr. Maryemma Graham, I recall comments on how the writer goes in and out of vogue but is never dismissed. Richard Wright is such a writer. His writings have overtly and covertly permeated the readership in America since the publication of *Native Son* in 1940. This is one of the major reasons scholars continuously discover and rediscover so many aspects of Wright's art to examine. This writer's texts hardly lose relevancy in a post modern world community so often challenged with socioeconomic and political issues—issues that all of his fiction addresses. His treatment of a historically racialized society and the fecundity of issues regarding race, sexuality, and violence in his texts give credence to his prophetic and relevant voice.

My study contributes to analyses that begin the process of dissecting Wright's narrative technique to cite patterns—the types of patterns and strategies he demonstrates in his characterizations and plot development, especially with the female character. Readers and scholars are familiar with how Wright treats this female character, but more critical in Wright scholarship is how that treatment comes about, that is, the *process* by which it occurs. An approach that investigates the writer's technique and strategy is one that takes the existing scholarship to another level of critical scrutiny. I was less interested in the "what" of the female's characterization, which valuable past studies have offered, but rather the "how" of it—how Wright manipulates and maneuvers the female character throughout the narrative structure.

By examining this pattern of use and discard with Wright's treatment of the female character, I have observed how he executes the development of dramatic conflict. Wright is exercising his study of writing fiction as a self-educated reader and writer rather than one who has been influenced by the study of texts in an academic setting. This type of scholarly and creative independence, apart from formal schooling, may account for this mechanistic, rather formulaic approach to writing fiction. Thus, by learning to write fiction as a technical craft, Wright demonstrates this tendency to effect drama and conflict in his narratives by designating a specific function of the female. The female character initiates the action, and Wright engages a process of design; this character will be the agent for creating the conflict that will result in the male character's process of victimization. Once this victimization of the male is embedded in the narrative structure, the female character exits the narrative; her significance has been replaced by a male counterpart. Therefore, by observing this pattern in Wright, one becomes more centered on his technique and strategy, a significant aspect of the writer's artistic style.

In addition, my research was enriched by reading alternative interpretations of how Wright presents the process of victimization with his male character. Thus, Neal A. Lester's article that uses the context of popular culture for analyzing Wright's minimally treated text, "The Man Who Killed a Shadow," was an inspiration. I acquired a keener interest in how Wright may be reinterpreted in the twenty first century. This theme and process of male victimization will continue to be reinterpreted and reevaluated, which often occurs with the Bigger Thomas character.

In addition, I am continuously awed at how gender specific some events are in real life in cases alleging violence and sexual assault on the part of

African American males against white females—the very stuff of Wright's fiction. By encountering sexuality via black and white relations in Wright's texts, and observing what can be perceived as widely publicized racialized sexual assault cases involving African American males and white females, the reader is constantly reminded of the interrelatedness of sex and racism in America. From Bigger's and Mary's connection in *Native Son* to the varied sexual fantasies and sexually-oriented brushes Fishbelly has with white females in Wright's later novel, *The Long Dream*, one observes a subject that Wright never ignored. Regarding this rather sensitive subject, Walker Alexander comments on Wright's marriages to two white females and other noted African Americans who had interracial marriages. According to this biographer, "C. L. James gives the most rational explanation--'Who else were we going to marry? (in the Communist Party). These were the girls who were available . . .'" (326).

As observed how Wright emphasizes the tragic fate of the African American male in connection to both white and African American female counterparts, I also observed that he cannot deviate from subjugating, negating, and disposing of the female character. In contrast, though Wright's male protagonists rarely survive, he presents them with such a sense of humanity and dignity that they acquire a tragic heroic stature. The autobiographical novel, *Black Boy*, other autobiographical sketches, such as "The Ethics of Living Jim Crow," and four major biographies, reveal the varied influences, too often racially and familially conflicting, that shape his art. Wright was familiar with the situation of interracial marriages and relationships, but more important, he was steeped in an understanding of race matters in his native country and abroad as a southern native son of color and as an expatriate living in France.

When *The Long Dream* was published in 1958, it was considered Wright's weakest text because of this expatriation in France. Critics cited the writer's distance from his subject matter, racism, and even setting, the South, where race relations were beginning to change. However, even current international events and crises in our global communities can be traced to being addressed in Wright's text, especially his prose. Terrorism and international conflicts involving the United States' and European nations' relations with the Arab nations are reflected either directly or indirectly in Wright's report on the 1955 Bandung Conference, compiled in a lesser known and read work, *The Color Curtain* (1956). The subject of American and European colonialism and neocolonialism was the agenda for this first formal gathering of leaders from what was then termed "Third World Nations." Moreover, undoubtedly, the race question, what W. E. Dubois terms, "the color line," continues to plague the United States and international communities. Therefore, Wright's relevancy in the context of race and international affairs cannot be denied.

Wright credits his mother as the one who initiates him into the world of fiction. His dedication to her in *Native Son* reads, "To my mother who, when I was a child at her knee, taught me to revere the fanciful and the imaginative." As stated in chapter one, his mother and another female, his cousin, introduced him to the world of fiction. Thus, the crucial status that females have in Wright's life is needed for the production of his art; they assist in its development. Wright's mother dies, and the female cousin is dismissed form the house because his religiously fanatical grandmother felt that by reading him fairy tales, she was introducing him to "the stuff of the devil." Thus, the concept of use and discard points to real life shapers. Finally, if one considers Houston Baker's comment, . . . "the autobiographical element is strong in all of Wright's work," then one becomes aware of Wright's motivation for using the female character as he does to emphasize the victimization of African American males. He makes an unquestionable contribution to American letters, and his fiction, especially in the context of gender, creates so many challenges that reveal his complexity and relevance in a postmodern world.